# THE INSIDE STORY OF THE WORLD'S TOUGHEST REGIMENT

# BOB CREW

# GURKHA WARRIORS

metro

Published by Metro Publishing Ltd,
3, Bramber Court, 2 Bramber Road,
London W14 9PB, England

First published in hardback in 2003

ISBN 1 84358 058 6

British Library Cataloguing-in-Publication Data:

A catalogue record for this book is available from the British Library.

Design by ENVY

Printed in Great Britain by CPD (Wales)

1 3 5 7 9 10 8 6 4 2

Papers used by Metro Publishing are natural, recyclable products made from wood grown in sustainable forests. The manufacturing processes conform to the environmental regulations of the country of origin.

Pictures reproduced by kind permission of Rex Features, the Gurkha Museum, Major Mark Austin, Royal Gurkha Rifles, Major Laxmi Bantawa and Brigadier Peter Pearson.

Every attempt has been made to contact the relevant copyright-holders, but some were unobtainable. We would be grateful if the appropriate people could contact us.

# DEDICATION

To Sean, Whose Generation Was Lucky
Enough to Escape Military Service, and to Pat
and Michele, Who Were Very Glad of It.

# CONTENTS

# ACKNOWLEDGEMENTS

This book is written with gratitude to all the people who have co operated with me in order to produce this historical and present-day profile of Britain's Gurkha soldiers and officers. I am grateful to them for entering into the spirit of things, granting their time and/or telling me their stories, both on and off record. Without their help, completing my task would have been much more difficult and time-consuming.

My special thanks go to: Major Mark Austin, formerly of the 10th Gurkha Rifles, for agreeing to be interviewed and arranging for me to attend his regiment's annual reunion at the Shorncliffe Barracks, in Kent, as a means of introduction to so many other British and Gurkha officers, including Rambahadur Limbu VC (also thanks to Mark for finding the time to vet Chapter 7, in which he and his colleagues are interviewed and profiled); Major

General Peter Pearson, for answering my questions and pointing me in the direction of others (he was Brigadier of the Royal Gurkha Rifles when I first met him, but has since been promoted and dispatched to Bosnia); Colonel Bill Dawson at Gurkha headquarters in Wiltshire, for agreeing to be interviewed, and for meeting me at the Gurkha Museum in Winchester and introducing me there (also for taking the trouble to point out notable sources and books to me and for vetting Chapter 8); Corporal Mulbir at Gurkha headquarters for dealing with my emails and sending me photographs; the curator and staff of the Gurkha Museum for permitting me to spend time there; Colonel Charles Wylie for taking time out of his retirement to be interviewed about his involvement in the first ascent of Mount Everest with Hillary, Hunt and Tenzing in 1953; all the British and Gurkha officers who readily conversed with me at the reunion of the 10th Gurkhas at the Shorncliffe Barracks (some of whom I have referred to and/or featured in these pages); the ethnic Gurkha officers of Gorkha origin with whom I sat and conversed over a splendid curry at the reunion; Major Laxmi Bantawa, for agreeing to be interviewed and telling me his story; the St James's Palace office of His Royal Highness the Prince of Wales, for co-operating with me on the subject of the relationship between Prince Charles and the Royal Gurkha Rifles, of which the Prince is Colonel-in-Chief, and for faxing me quotes from the Prince for publication in this book (special thanks to Mands Foster); the librarian at the London Library, who sent me so many books and waited patiently for their overdue return; Nick Martin of Halifax-Equitable for introducing me to Major Mark Austin in the first place; the publisher John Blake, for having 'looked for a book on the Gurkhas for some time now' and for inviting me to write it; and anyone else whom I have inadvertently overlooked.

# INTRODUCTION

To recount the colourful and adventurous 186-year history of the Gurkhas is a rare gift for any writer. It is a glittering prize, for theirs is the extraordinary story of a legendary people whose astonishing exploits echo down through the ages. Nor is there any shortage of material from which to choose in setting out the history of these amazing and at times mind-boggling soldiers. As we know from the Gurkha Museum in Winchester, 'keeping the peace in India under the British flag began for Gurkha soldiers ... in 1817 ... and the first battle honour gained by Gurkha troops was ... in 1826'. A lot of water has gone under the bridge since then, and a lot of blood and guts have been spilled on too many battlefields.

But I have not attempted to offer a detailed and precise

1

military history here. There are already plenty of such books gathering dust in regimental and other libraries. Instead I have chosen to turn my pen to a story of adventure and one that reflects the changing role of the Gurkhas in the service of the British Army from one generation to the next. In so doing I have tried to capture the spirit, atmosphere and people of different periods during the long and romantic relationship between Britain and its Gurkha soldiers. I have sought to breathe new life into a story that has been tackled by a great many writers before me.

When revisiting the hallowed ground of the Gurkhas' past, one cannot fail to respect what has gone before and to strive to do justice to it. But at the same time one is also aware of the need to bring the story up to date with some new and more modern insights, shedding new light where possible and exploring how today's Gurkhas are perceived in the new millennium. All of this I have tried to do by looking at how royalty, academics and other soldiers (including enemy soldiers) have perceived the Gurkhas, while also considering how some of today's ethnic Gurkha officers perceive themselves and their country, and how their white officers perceive them.

The chances are that this is the first military book to include ethnic Gurkha voices (other military books have had plenty of photographed faces, but not voices). It is also the first military book to resist the temptation of looking at the Gurkhas exclusively from the narrow military standpoint of the white officer class, and, as a result, ethnic Gurkha soldiers can be seen in a new light.

The inclusion of ethnic voices in a military book is an important 'first' for Gurkha communities in Britain, Nepal and other parts of the world. Previously these soldiers have been written about by their (white) superior officers, but in this book they are breaking new ground and getting themselves heard at last; getting themselves included for the first time in the shaping and telling of a story about them. There is much more to be done in this regard in future books, but at least a start has been made here.

It is also likely that this is the first book to have published a poem in celebration of the Gurkhas as a prelude to their story. My poem is a studied imitation and mild paraphrase of a similar poem that T.E. Lawrence wrote to romanticise the Arabs in 1926 and stamp them firmly into the pages of English literature, in *Seven Pillars of Wisdom*, a book which, by Lawrence's own admission, did 'not pretend to be impartial' and was intended as a highly 'personal narrative pieced out of memory'.

The object of imitating the Lawrence poem is not to parody it, but to make a point about the representation of history, and turn the tide of that history in favour of the Gurkhas for a change, since they have always been far more important to British interests and victories than Arab warriors. For this reason it defies belief that a *Lawrence of Arabia*-type film has not been made about Britain's Gurkha soldiers, whose colourful and exciting story has been every bit as thrilling, intriguing and politically decisive in the affairs of the British Empire as that of the Arabs (the chief differences being that the Gurkhas have not had scholarly white Arabists to adore them and oil has not been a consideration).

Finally, this book would seem to be the first to have the uninterrupted and unedited voice of Prince Charles on the subject of the Gurkhas. Other books on the Gurkhas do not quote the Prince at such length or at all – on the contrary he is generally mentioned, if at all, only in passing - yet his views are not without interest, since they are not generally known outside Gurkha military circles, and he is the Gurkhas' Colonel-in-Chief. When profiling the Gurkha officer class in Britain – ethnic and white – it makes sense to include the Prince of Wales in this context, and to give prominence to his views, which are of interest, not only in Britain, but also in the wider Gurkha world, which includes Nepal, India and Brunei. So then, at least three modest firsts in honour of our Gurkha friends.

Not that the Gurkhas are unaccustomed to firsts. They have a long and creditable list of them to their name. These include being: the first into Tibet and Hunza in the days when these mysterious places were dangerous no-go areas; the first to encounter the 'Russian Bear' and the Cossacks in a highly sensitive and politically explosive Central Asia in the days of Kipling's 'Great Game'; the first Asian soldiers to have a short story devoted to them by Rudyard Kipling, who wrote 'In the Presence' in their honour; among the first soldiers who fought the highest skirmish in military history, at 18,500 feet in Tibet (as well as the first, this may well be the last such skirmish); the first Asian soldiers to clock up the greatest number of VCs during the Second World War (ten out of twenty-six); the first and only Asian soldiers to be among those who helped to conquer Mount Everest in the days when it was still worth conquering (led by a white British Gurkha officer who is interviewed in this book); the first Asian soldiers to become honorary Europeans; and the first and only Asian regiment to receive a royal prefix for the impressive way that it policed the North-West Frontier in the days of the Raj.

So the Gurkhas really are no strangers to firsts, and it has been my pleasure to record these and other accomplishments, not least because most readers will probably be unaware of these fascinating but lesser-known facts.

Because there are many different ways of looking at Britain's Gurkha soldiers, I have gone to some trouble to view them from different angles: not just as the world-beating soldiers everybody agrees that, with others, they obviously are, but also as outstanding mountain climbers; and, in more recent times, as a new breed of ethnic officers and gentlemen in their own right. One cannot do full justice to the Gurkhas, as both extraordinary men of war and remarkable human beings, without looking at them from all these different angles.

And, at a time when so many more of them are being pensioned off than in previous years – when fewer and fewer are being recruited, because the British Army is shrinking fast – it is also impossible to do full honour to the Gurkhas without extending to them the gratitude that these courageous men so richly deserve.

They deserve a golden handshake, of course, but like so

many of their white counterparts in the long history of the British Army, it doesn't look as though they are going to get one. They are 'the poor bloody infantry' after all. But what an infantry!

And, notwithstanding the fickle nature of courage and the paradox of the basic dualism of human nature that is forever part hero and part coward (subjects also dealt with in this book), how rich they are in humanity and soldierly virtues. Here's to them all.

## TO JOHNNY GURKHA

*We admired and respected you, so we drew tides of*
*your men into our hands and wrote your will with*
*ours across the sky in blood and gun smoke*
*To earn us freedom and you a modest house under the*
*stars so that your moonlit eyes might be shining for us*
*When we came.*

*Death cast its ever-present shadow across our*
*uninviting road, but when we drew near*
*and saw you waiting*
*With your unrelenting smile, and heard the steady*
*drum-beat of your courageous heart*
*with which to take death apart,*
*We feared death no more.*

*But when death and injury savaged your body*
*with ours and we bore it together as one flesh*
*between two, sunny side up,*

## INTRODUCTION

*Before the hungry earth swallowed us*
*both and fed well on our substance,*
*then we went to ground*
*Together.*

*When death groped our hearts and souls to have its*
*wicked way with the two of us*
*We shared that monstrous fear without*
*shedding a single tear of blood,*
*dying where we stood*
*In sweet memory of each other.*

*With two differently cultured and pigmented*
*skins with which to win*
*so many impossible battles*
*We left our mark here, there, and everywhere*
*for all with the eyes to see*
*that the difference between us*
*Was and remains minimal*

*Except that it was we who had most of the freedom*
*and all of the power,*
*leaving the little that was left of the equation to you.*
*But what else, in the circumstances, could either of us do?*
*What could we have done*
*to have altered history's sum?*

## one

# LOVE AT FIRST FRIGHT

When British and Gurkha soldiers first clapped eyes on one another, they did so as deadly foes, in two long and bloody military campaigns in the Anglo-Nepalese war of 1814-16, and it was love at first sight – and fright.

Fighting with a passion, in the blood-curdling heat of battle, they sought out one another's fear, eyeball to eyeball. In hand-to-hand fighting, with bayonet and the famous Gurkha *kukri* – a sharp, curved knife that can also be used as a miniature sword – the British liked and esteemed what they saw on the darker side of life in the foothills of what is now west Nepal.

They had come with the aim of defeating a dangerous enemy who were likewise spoiling for an all-out fight. But before long these fearsome rivals had developed a mutual soldierly infatuation based on an admiration for one another's fighting qualities.

9

As the Honourable C.G. Bruce, the legendary nineteenth-century British commander of the 1/5th Gurkha Regiment, observed in his book *The Gurkhas*: 'It was … an eye-opener to our army in India to find another race which … could meet them and beat them on equal terms.'

But the British did not take defeat lying down. They went straight back and conquered their foe. By the time a further very fierce battle was over, the Gurkhas were congratulating the British, as Lieutenant John Shipp recounted in *The Path of Glory – The Memoirs of the Extraordinary Career of John Shipp*: 'As we moved off this young stranger shook me warmly by the hand, saying, "I love a brave soldier, and all white men are brave." He was, it appeared, the Adjutant of the corps in which Khissna Rhannah, the man I killed, was Colonel.'

In writing this book I have met many ethnic Gurkha officers who, nearly two centuries later, still echo this sentiment. Among them is Major Laxmi Bantawa of the Royal Gurkha Rifles in Britain, who told me: 'British soldiers are the best in the world… Everybody knows it.' Praise indeed from soldiers who are themselves among the very best in the world.

The British met other races, too, who gave them a good run for their money – Sikhs and Pathans spring to mind – but here was a brown-skinned race that was astonishingly like the British in some not unimportant ways.

In his book *Warrior Gentlemen – 'Gurkhas' in the Western Imagination*, Lionel Caplan, Professor of Anthropology at the University of London's School of Oriental and African Studies, tells us: 'All fighting groups in the Indian army shared at least some of the characteristics of their officers, who of course embodied the quintessence of the martial ideal. But the Gurkhas seemed to have an additional quality associated with those who led them: that special combination of traits (courtesy, humour, sportsmanship) which defines persons of breeding. They were, in short, not simply warriors, but gentlemen as well; hence their depiction as akin to public school boys. Their exoticism therefore lay not in their foreignness, but paradoxically in their very likeness to the officers who led them. Despite being "Easterners," they possessed the most desirable qualities of western (European) civilised culture. The Gurkhas thus reflected back the officers' own image of themselves as men of honour and refinement. There was certainly no desire on the part of the military authors to represent the Gurkhas as the very antithesis of themselves… These soldiers were … embraced as honorary Europeans.'

There is something to be said for this view, but it is not the whole story, because there were other things about the Gurkhas that were very foreign indeed, and not in the least European, and this was clearly recognised and understood by both the white British officers who recruited them and the British soldiers who fought alongside them.

When the British first encountered the Gurkhas, the latter had animist and other religious and superstitious beliefs that were not at all like Christian beliefs. They also kept slave boys, decapitated their enemies in combat – as well as severing the heads of goats and buffalo for religious purposes (which they do to this day) – and they believed in ghosts and had a passion for spicy curry. All of this has been written about and none of it marks them out as being akin to Lionel Caplan's British public school boys or honorary Europeans. While British officers who wrote about the Gurkhas admired the gentlemanly and manly Gurkha traits that most resembled the qualities of the British, they did not turn a blind eye to these other 'strange' things about the Gurkhas. For example, Lieutenant Shipp tells us in his memoirs that in the first wars against the Gurkhas, the Gurkha soldier fought 'under the banner of gloomy superstition; cruelty is their creed, and murder of their foes the zenith of their glory'.

From the start, military literature reflected characteristics of the Gurkhas that had little in common with their British masters, in addition to describing those qualities that they did have in common – a good sense of humour, courtesy, bravery and sportsmanship. And while there was an emphasis put on the latter, the former certainly did not pass without comment or explanation. Unlike many other white races, the British, for reasons of diplomacy or otherwise, generally respected or at least tolerated aspects of racial and cultural difference that they did not understand or approve of. Their view seems to have been that life is short and that it was not part of their game plan to change people psychologically or culturally, or punch them on the nose for their racial differences; they preferred, if they could, to win hearts and minds by not interfering too much with the customs of others.

In particular, the severing of enemy heads was not a typically British or European practice in the nineteenth century – although it had been much earlier in European history, when many a head was contemptuously spiked for gruesome display before such grisly acts of retribution were abandoned. So the Gurkhas' headhunting had nothing to do with the public-school ethos to which Caplan refers. Nor was it likely to scare the British, who knew all about such savagery from their own history. It was unlikely that the Gurkhas, or any other race for that matter, could tell the British anything about violence and barbarism that they didn't know or hadn't experienced already.

As for the Gurkha soldier today, Colonel Bill Dawson of the Royal Gurkha Rifles in Britain, has told me: 'There is no culture among Gurkha soldiers of collecting heads. No cult of headhunting. Gurkhas are not like that at all. The Japanese used ritual beheading as a form of execution, but not the Gurkhas. The Gurkhas are very honourable in their treatment of prisoners. In the days of the musket or bolt-action rifle, Gurkha soldiers simply found it more natural to get their *kukris* out than to fix a bayonet as an extension to a rifle, or when they had run out of bullets. They used the *kukri* merely as a method that they were used to. The head coming off was incidental. It has nothing to do with paganism or Hinduism of the plains of India. The Gurkhas really are very honourable in their treatment of prisoners. They have this fearsome reputation, but they are the most gentle people, providing, of course, you remember not to wind them up or make them too angry! The Gurkhas are a hardy and self-sufficient breed of people because they come from communities separated by fast-flowing rivers, so they find it difficult to get out during the months of May, June, July and August, when the Himalayan melt in the hot monsoon season pours down the mountains, causing landslides and deaths, cutting off one village and tribe from another.'

Shipp tells us that, when the Gurkhas first set eyes on the British, they thought them to be 'Devils rather than men, who had dropped down upon them from the skies. Some of them even believed that we had been seen passing through the air in flying carriages, drawn by celestial elephants; until a few, who were braver than the rest, had a good look at us and exploded the superstition. They were astounded that we had climbed that terrific mountain, indeed, looking at it afterwards, we wondered ourselves how we had managed to get an army up it, equipped too with twenty-four pounder guns… It was now twenty hours since I had eaten… I had no bedding and could not sleep… It was dark and lonely.'

When the British first came up against the Gurkhas, two expanding empires were on a collision course. One was Asian and not in the least powerful in global terms, the other Anglo-Saxon and increasingly powerful both globally and in British India, where the Asian empire of the Gurkhas was a thorn in the flesh of the Anglo-Saxon empire.

The little Asian empire builders thought nothing of invading others' territory in their own neck of the woods, while Britain's empire builders were a long way from home and thought nothing of being there (even though they were swatted like flies, not just on the field of battle, but also by ghastly ill-health and devastating diseases, as well as, of course, insanity in the noonday sun).

Born out of ferocious violence and bloodshed, deadly serious bravery and extraordinary heroics, the irresistible love affair between the British and the Gurkhas is one of the most psychologically intriguing and astonishing stories known to military history. It is of interest not only to soldiers and historians, but also to psychologists, and to members of the general public on whose behalf British and Gurkha soldiers are still sent to spill their own and others' blood in the four corners of our deeply troubled world.

If it is possible to perceive the Gurkhas as 'honorary Europeans' in British eyes, it is also possible to perceive some of the British as 'honorary Gurkhas'. John Shipp, for example, became a Gurkha in many respects. A hard and expendable life had led him to join the British Army at nine years of age, whereupon he found himself a subordinate to the officer class, fighting in foreign lands, including Africa, where, in the absence of shoes, he had to cut buffalo hide to fit the soles of his feet when he went into battle. This illiterate orphan from Saxmundham, in Suffolk, who had been brought up in a workhouse and had to teach himself how to read and write, worked his way up through the ranks of the army to become 'an officer and a gentleman'. Yet, for all the disadvantage and backwardness in his harsh life, he remained amazingly cheerful and optimistic, and he finished up reading Shakespeare, the Bible and many of the plays of his time, as well as teaching himself Hindustani and interpreting on behalf of his friends and colleagues. One's heart goes out to the likes of Shipp, who was as brave and tough as any Gurkha he came up against (yet was able to better himself and improve his mind whilst spilling other people's guts on the field of battle!)

As C.J. Stranks points out, in his introduction to Shipp's

memoirs, while a long list of educated viceroys, generals and civil servants have written accounts of their experiences in India and Nepal in those far-off times, Shipp became 'one of the very few private soldiers who have put into print what it was like to be one of the valiant, inarticulate, expendable many on whom the whole structure of authority rested. That of itself was a considerable feat.' He adds: 'They were remarkable men, that handful of soldiers and civilians who, more by force of circumstance than design, spread British power throughout India. In Shipp's day Kipling's Army of India was in the making... The ordinary soldier, once he arrived in the country, had only a small chance of getting home again. Disease, the climate, battle … made such an event extremely unlikely.'

Stranks believes that while 'every detail' in Shipp's memoirs 'may not be correct', the overall picture that he presents 'is authentic beyond doubt'. And what a picture it is. Shipp tells us: 'We were not in this wild country just for sport. We were there to conquer an artful and warlike people, whose triumphs over us the year before had made them overbearing in the extreme. They laughed at any idea of a settlement, and trusted, with good reason, to the almost inaccessible nature of their country... They seemed to be solely on the defensive... The fighting soon became very warm, for the enemy maintained their ground manfully. I hate a runaway foe, for there is no credit in beating him, but these were no flinchers. I never saw a steadier bravery than they showed in all my life. Run they would not, death held no terrors for them... Thus ended the fighting in the second campaign, in what has been called the Goorka War... Our complete victory ... beat some new principles into our foes.'

Pale-faced British soldiers had come from the other end of the earth – the far side of the moon as far as the Gurkhas were concerned – and they were ready to spill the blood of Gurkhas and any others who got in their way. But they soon realised that they had one hell of a fight on their hands as these tough little men introduced them to gallons of their own blood.

Ten years after Robert Clive's victory at the Battle of Plassey in 1757, which established Britain's imperial supremacy in India, the British became increasingly aware of a settlement north-west of Kathmandu called Gorkha, and it is this ancient and legendary place, steeped in mythology, from which the incomparable Gurkha takes his name.

Today Gorkha is a small and unspectacular town, but in those far-off times it was a place notorious for its war-mongering. The mere mention of its name sent shudders down the spines of its neighbours, because the cruel Gurkhas were making a big and nightmarish nuisance of themselves, spreading terror far and wide, under the leadership of Prithvi Narayan Shah. This king reigned over a backward hill state that had less than 12,000 households, lacked resources or industry of its own and was cut off from the outside world and ignored by the trade routes. Yet Prithvi Narayan Shah had built up a mighty arsenal of arms and was hell-bent on invading his neighbours and grabbing their land in order to find a way out of his kingdom's poverty.

Prithvi Shah is reported to have asked the direction of Nepal and Kathmandu, and the thought came to his heart that he might be its king. What a thought and what a heart.

No one doubted that the Gurkhas were all heart. Brave heart, cold heart, hard heart, warm and generous and big heart. But what about their heads? Where would their king's vision take them?

Eventually the visionary and dynamic Prithvi, who did not know which city was which in the Kathmandu Valley, conquered it. With a regular army of no fewer than 15,000 soldiers – and a great many more irregulars as and when he needed them – he fought long and hard for twenty-five years in order to do so. In a series of bloody assaults and military campaigns, he cut off the trade routes of his neighbours and enforced an economic blockade on the valley. It was when the trade routes were threatened that the Gorkas' terrified neighbours turned to the British for help. But the first British expeditionary force seriously underestimated the nature of the challenge and was in consequence cut to pieces in their first ever encounter with the Gurkhas, while others of their number had already died of malaria en route to the field of battle. Of course, the Gurkhas knew more about fighting in the hills and mountains than the British, and it showed.

To this day the Gurkhas believe that they were the founders of the modern state of Nepal. After the British defeated the Prithvi Narayan Shah dynasty and started to take those of his troops who volunteered to join the British ranks, they very sensibly left Nepal to run its own affairs as a nominally independent country while they got on with the business of taking and holding British India.

So this is how the Gurkhas and the British first met. And

these events explain why the Gurkhas – who, as soldiers of fortune, had already sold their services to other armies, notably the Sikhs – decided to enlist with the British, who have since that time marvelled at the Gurkhas' uncomplaining indifference to death and danger, neither of which seems to hold any fears for them.

Perhaps we should not be surprised by the Gurkhas' fearlessness in the face of death. If you come from an extremely harsh country with hardly any roads and almost no welfare, housing or unemployment aid (most of which problems persist in Nepal to this day), a country in which natural disasters such as landslides and earthquakes are commonplace, you may well not value life particularly highly or be afraid of death, since life has always been, for as long as you can remember, fundamentally cold-hearted, bleak, uninviting and cruel. Why would you fear death when you have such little to lose? And when you have given up complaining long ago, because you have learnt that it gets you nowhere at all. Instead, you accept your fate, as you shrug off hardship and even death itself, and simply keep your head down and make your own fiercely independent way in life, overcoming all odds with endurance, fortitude and patience in the hostile environment in which you find yourself.

And, when you have managed to rise above the dire and luckless circumstances of your life as a Gurkha by digging deep into your inner resources and unfailing sense of humour, the chances are that you may be somewhat proud of yourself for having withstood such an unenviable life with dignity and even a smile, for having proved yourself and kept faith with yourself in the face of a wretched fate that has never shown you a single kindness or done anything other than glare in your direction (if looks could kill!). So this is where Gurkha pride and rigorously tested self-belief come from, and without an unrelenting sense of self-belief, how else would you survive all this, when life itself seems not to believe in you very much, when fortune refuses to smile on you? And if you happen to subscribe to a religion that accentuates your self-belief, well then, so much the better. And if you come from one of the deep valleys that demands an arduous climb if you are to get out of it and is cut off from neighbouring valeys once a year when the Himalayan ice melts and ferocious rivers swell up and encircle your valley, causing landslides, how could you have not become a highly self-sufficient person?

Given all this – and favourable DNA to provide you with the necessary release of those adrenaline hormones when faced with fear and danger – you may very well have the makings of a good Gurkha soldier. Because such a soldier must be endowed with not only all the rugged human qualities and military virtues, but also a strong need for the sense of 'family' that the army can supply when your own family is poor and unable to provide for you, it stands to reason that the Gurkha soldiers qualify in this respect also. So, when the British Army comes along and smiles in your direction, responding to your fate as well as your social handicap and soldierly qualities, showing you every courtesy and respect, and offering you comradeship and a family of sorts – and when it is an army that you can in turn respond to and respect – why would you not join it? Why would it not become, for you, life itself, offering you a home and the chance to master (rather than endure) your own fate for a change? There is, of course, no reason why you would not join such an army and put your life, such as it is, on the line for it. And while, in this day and age, the paternalism of the British officer class for its Gurkha soldiers is no longer as strong as it once was, it is still part of the picture. Moreover, because you come from a community in which, since the age of ten, you have been sent from your tumbledown hillside shack to stay up in the hills for weeks or even months on end, looking after the family's goats, you may well be rather more mature and hard-headed than other boy soldiers, and perhaps physically fitter and stronger too.

When the first Gurkha soldiers enlisted with the British East India Company Army, they were keeping slave boys who had been conscripted into the Gurkha army. These boys served as camp followers, carrying arms and baggage, building stockades and undertaking menial tasks in return for their keep until such time as they could become soldiers too, after they had served their apprenticeship and been trained by their Gurkha masters.

In *Imperial Warriors*, an excellent book by the former British Gurkha officer Tony Gould, Major Frederick Young, who served as a thirty-year-old lieutenant in the Gurkha war of the early nineteenth century, is reported as saying in the Bengal Military Consultations back in December 1829: 'It never was the custom of the Chiefs of the Gorkha Army on the North West Frontier to entertain raw recruits from the conquered states. These boys had to be trained and to prove themselves as hardy and amenable to discipline on active service as their masters were, before they could even be considered as soldiers.' Young took the view that it was this gruelling apprenticeship of slave boys that led to 'the superiority of the Gorkha army over any other with which the British power has come into contact'. This belief in the Gurkhas' superiority was shared by, among many others, the Nepal-based British diplomat Brian Hodgson, who has described them as 'by far the best soldiers in Asia' who, as 'participators of our renown in arms' could be 'relied on for fidelity'. (However, as the Gurkhas would no doubt be the first to concede, the Japanese, Sikhs and mixed-race Anglo-Indians also occupy the top of the Asian military league.)

One of the reasons why the Gurkha army generally terrified anyone who dared to cross it was that its soldiers seemed to enjoy nothing more than beheading their enemies and slicing or cutting off the noses and lips of those whom they captured. When Kirtipur fell to the Gurkhas, some 865 noses were reportedly severed, including the noses and lips of all males over the age of twelve. There were reports of Gurkha soldiers running back from the field of battle with their *kukris* in one hand and, in the other, a clutch of severed heads to be kept as trophies. It was an army that oppressed and sometimes enslaved defeated people, using them as forced labour, so the British took a deep breath and decided that enough was enough. But what to do about such a terrifying mob? They would have to put their foot down against these little Nepalese men with big ambitions. But little did they realise what they were letting themselves in for.

All this was a very long time ago, before the British had wised up to military matters out East and in unaccustomed terrain, and got themselves world-beating parachute, marine commando and SAS regiments. They had their crack infantry and cavalry regiments, certainly, but they still had plenty to learn in the global theatre of war, not least in Asia, which held many surprises and terrors for them and other Western powers who ventured there. (Unlike the Americans, generations later in Vietnam, the British learnt their lessons and learnt them well.) So there was no way that the British Army, or anyone else, was going to crush the Gurkhas, because the notion of military defeat was not part of the Gurkha mindset. On the contrary, it was these short, stocky, brown- or olive-skinned men who were accustomed to doing the crushing; terrifying little combatants who would take off the enemy's head with their *kukris* as soon as look at him.

In the years that followed, the Gurkhas impressed the above-mentioned Major Frederick Young as follows: 'They are generally short, light bodied, well limbed men, well calculated to bear fatigue, particularly in a Hill Country, they are fiery in dispute, fond to a fault of Gambling, full of energy, and sanguine in all their undertakings. They are naturally slovenly in their dress, but I consider them smart, intelligent and brave soldiers, attached to their officers … with an almost instinctive sense of the necessity for discipline. In disposition they are loyally attached to the British Service to which they look for protection. They are at the same time proud of the name of Gorkahs, which carries with it recollections of Martial deeds. They look down on the regular Native Sepoys, to whom they consider themselves superior, but they have the highest opinion of the Europeans as soldiers, and respect their courage, and discipline, and whenever they have been associated with European Troops, a Mutual good understanding and the best of feeling has existed.'

Young took the view that the Gurkha army had 'nobly defended itself' against the British.

But something of a shadow was cast over these first favourable impressions of the Gurkhas by the British officer class when Father Guiseppe, a prefect of the Roman Mission in Nepal, wrote in his *An Account of the Kingdom of Nepal* that 'at the beginning of 1769, it was a most horrid spectacle to behold so many people hanging on trees in the road'.

And, again, after the Gurkha ruler Prithvi Narayan Shah ordered his soldiers to cut off the noses and lips of those who surrendered to him Kirtipur, which he renamed the City of Cut-Noses (Naskatapur), the priest recorded that it was 'shocking to see so many living people with their teeth and noses resembling the skulls of the deceased'. Father Giuseppe was not alone in his predictable horror. A Briton, Captain Kirkpatrick, likewise recorded his disgust at the absence of so many noses.

However, James Baillie Fraser tells us in *Journal of a Tour* that, 'whatever the nature of the Ghoorkhas may have been found in other quarters', when it came to the British, 'there was no cruelty to wounded or prisoners … no rancorous spirit of revenge seemed to animate them: they fought us in fair conflict, like men; and in the intervals of actual combat, showed us a liberal courtesy worthy of a more enlightened people.'

If this was true, then it would seem that the Gurkhas were as spellbound by the British as the latter were spellbound by them, and that it was either the case that the Gurkhas reserved their best treatment for the British, or that the British brought out the best in the Gurkhas. Either way, the relationship was an improving one, and the mutual-admiration society seemed to be prospering.

Of course, it took fearless men with nerves of steel to tangle with the lethal Gurkhas, and for the officers of the British East India Company Army and their British and Indian troops, who were the first to do this, it was without doubt a dark time. They had to keep their wits about them, be diligent and make a brave fist of it, if they were to come out of the encounter alive, and with their noses and lips intact after hand-to-hand fighting with the Gurkha foe. For the Gurkhas were all the more skilled with their *kukris* because, apart from mutilating the enemy with them, they used them to butcher buffalo and other animals in peace time, as well as to hack wood, and then to ceremonially slaughter hundreds of goats and buffalo in religious rituals in which the higher the blood spurted, the more blessings from the gods the sacrifice was supposed to produce. The Gurkhas have always been unafraid of the sight of blood and perhaps this is not surprising in view of their religion and the harsh necessities of life in a community in which, traditionally, every other person has been a butcher, regularly cutting up livestock. Perhaps, when the cause is right, it is only a short step from the regular domestic and ritual butchery of animals to that of humans. But it is important to stress that the Gurkhas of yesteryear, whom the British military came so greatly to admire, are no more like today's Gurkhas than the Britons of yesteryear are like the people of modern Britain.

# two

# JOHNNY GURKHA IN BRITISH INDIA

Most Britons today are at least vaguely aware of 'Johnny Gurkha', with his broad-brimmed boy scout's hat, because his reputation has gone before him in the many battlefields around the world where he has served the British Crown. A man of popular myth, steeped in mystical glory, he has caught the romantic and sometimes lurid imagination of the masses. But most people do not know how Johnny Gurkha first came into contact with the British. They do not know the courageous and gory detail, the sacrifice and generosity, or the extraordinary spirit and character of the amazing man behind the Gurkha image.

Nor do most people realise that a great many Gurkhas are of Indian descent. These claim to be Rajputs who fled their Indian homeland in AD 1300, when Muslim empire builders were invading India. The Rajputs took off to the Himalayan foothills to build an impenetrable fortress refuge for themselves, where they retained their Hindu religion with its classical and priestly Brahmin caste system, in which Shatriya (warriors) supported the priesthood and Vaisya (merchants), while Sudras (Untouchables) were used as menials.

While some Gurkhas have Chinese or Mongolian features and are indeed of Mongolian descent, others have Indian or Burmese features, and some of them are olive- rather than brown-skinned. The latter group, born-again Brahmins and Rajputs, had overlords who unashamedly maintained the wide gap between rulers and ruled, rich and poor, in the kingdom of the House of Gorkha. Here, hopelessly and cruelly beyond the *terai* (lushly forested plain) of the Kathmandu Valley on which the Gurkha kingdom had set its sights, most people found it hard to scratch even a feeble living out of the barren hills. Life was harsh for these long-suffering people, who were products not only of their genes but also of a fiercely unrelenting landscape and a cruel social environment. But, somehow, they had learnt not to complain.

Professor Lionel Caplan writes: 'Linguistic and other evidence suggests that the earliest migrations originated from areas to the north of the kingdom, from the mountains of China, Burma, or Tibet. These "Mongoloid" people spoke a diversity of what are now classified as Tibeto-Burman languages, some virtually indistinguishable from one other, others mutually unintelligible… by the early middle ages, when new migrations from (mainly north) India began, these ethnic, or, as they are frequently labelled, "tribal" groups, had long been settled throughout the middle hills of what is now Nepal Himalaya.'

Caplan adds: 'The overwhelming majority of Gurkhas originate from the villages and townships situated within the middle hills of Nepal (the *pahar*), a territory roughly 500 miles in length (from west to east) and 80 miles in depth (from south to north). These hills, broken by deep river valleys, lie between the *terai*, a narrow belt of low-lying plains bordering India, and the high Himalayan ranges. The bulk of their inhabitants – who comprise perhaps sixty per cent of Nepal's population today, as a much higher proportion until relatively recently – reside in altitudes between 3,500 or 9,000 feet... recruitment into the Gurkhas has concentrated on only four ... groups ... namely the Magars, Garuns, Rais and Limbus.'

Even allowing for discrepancies in chronicled accounts – either of Rajput migration to Nepal or indeed of the number of Gurkha soldiers thrown into battle in the service of the British in different parts of the world – a strong picture emerges of remarkable mixed-race warring tribes, apparently of mixed Mongolian, Tibetan, Burmese and Indian descent that, in the fullness of time, fought more battles for the British than they did for themselves, both in the Indian sub-continent and in the world at large. A picture also emerges of a lost tribe of India, finding itself up in the hills and eventually under a British flag. Colonel Dawson takes the view that most of the 'Rajput stock has gone into the ruling classes'.

Having been originally driven into the hills by overwhelming numbers of Muslim invaders by whom they were excluded from their homeland – and then found themselves trapped between them (and later on the British) and mainland China, which was equally hostile to them – they found themselves between a rock and a hard place, so they got used to and made the most of it.

The story of the Gurkhas as a fighting force in the service of the British is astonishing and gruesome, and one can imagine how strange it must have seemed to the British soldiers in Nepal when it all began almost two centuries ago. Lieutenant Shipp tells us that 'in this paradise of beauty dwelt a cruel and barbarous people, proverbial for their bloody deeds, whose hearts were more callous than the flinty rocks that reared their majestic heads above their woody mountains. They are more savage in their nature than the hungry tiger that prowls through their dreary glens: cruel as the vulture; cold-hearted as their snowy mountains; subtle and cunning as the fiend of night; powerful as the rocks on which they live; and active as the goat upon the mountain's brow.'

And the paradise in question revealed: 'Nature's masterpiece of scenery. It was a little world of golden woods, which would have defied the skill of any artist to depict. The hills glittered in the rising sun, clear brooks fell from rock to rock, among great pines; the water, sometimes a cataract, sometimes no more than a gentle stream. Weeping willows leaned over the pools, with multitudes of fish playing in their shadow. All along the banks were roses, tulips, violets, and the air was filled with the song of birds. It was tragic that human blood should be shed there.' One would think that this romantic scene was the setting for a picnic rather than a battle.

Shipp was no slouch himself when it came to single-handed combat with Gurkha soldiers. Quoting from the first volume of Henry Prinsep's *History of Political and Military Translations in India, 1813–23*, Tony Gould tells us: '[Shipp's] weapon broke early in the conflict, whereupon he threw it away, and trusting to his activity, closed with the Goorkha, and wrenching his sword from him, laid him lifeless with a back-handed stroke. Feats of this kind are not the proper duty of officers, but when they occur are very encouraging to the troops; for the union of personal prowess with gallantry and success will always command admiration.'

Obviously Johnny Gurkha had inflamed the British imagination in such a way that he was rapidly becoming all things to all men. He was proving to be a wild farrago of a man, capable of all manner of contradictory things in mesmerised British eyes. One very appealing legendary story concerns Lieutenant Frederick Young. When the Gurkhas took Young prisoner and asked him why he had not run off when his Indian irregulars had deserted him in panic in the face of a ferocious *kukri*-wielding attack from the advancing Gurkhas, leaving him to be hacked to pieces and perhaps beheaded, the super-cool British lieutenant is said to have replied in a matter-of-fact way that he had not come into the hills to run away. Whereupon, General Sir Francis Tuker tells us in his book *Gorkha*, that the Gurkhas, who could speak some English, were so impressed by Young that they responded with warmth and admiration, 'We could serve under men like you.'

This story has been disputed by some – even whether Young was ever taken prisoner – but it is worth remembering that tales of this kind were and remain as popular with Gurkhas as they were and remain with the British, so it is hard to dismiss them either as complete nonsense or as irrelevant. The fact that they endure as the stuff of legend, with the cheerful approval of both sides, shows what both sides wanted to, and did, think about one another. It also shows that such stories, which may or may not be entirely truthful or factual, have an inner truth and underlying relevance that is entirely true to the spirit of their times. Indeed they still circulate and make good sense today, reflecting the mutual admiration that existed then and has continued to exist between Gurkha and British fighting men today. Such stories also speak volumes of the mutual expectations that grew out of this mutual esteem. All in all they reveal the true spirit and character of the relationship, which is no small consideration when one is seeking to arrive at the historical and psychological truth about the two races, both of whom combined bravery and romance with a deadly sense of humour.

Another story circulating about Johnny Gurkha at this time tells of a Gurkha who had part of his jaw shot away by the British at the siege of Lalanga during the first of the two military campaigns. He startled the British by appealing to them for medical aid and, once they had patched him up, he begged them to let him return to his own side so that he could continue the fight – which they did. There are stories of invading Gurkha soldiers running up steep mountain slopes and hillsides on all fours – faster than galloping horses, having done this all their lives in their hillside villages in Nepal – with a sharp flat knife in their mouths as they go in for the kill. And there are stories about them hanging upside down from the branches of trees to slice off the enemy's head while he is taken unawares as he passes beneath.

There are also tales of Gurkha women – some of whom were widows who had lost their husbands in battle, while others were camp women – who were allowed into army depots to comfort their men, and there are the inevitable stories about homosexual relationships between British officers and Gurkha soldiers during sexually lean times in remote places. And then there are stories of Gurkhas of Mongolian stock who adopted the name of their tribe as their surname, as a result of which scores of them shared the same surname when they enlisted with the British, even though they were quite unrelated, and who all took one pace forward together when a single name was called by their officers.

Stories about the Gurkhas' sense of humour include one in which they decided to take some armed Tibetans soldiers prisoner by tying their pigtails together while they were asleep. Disturbed in this act of comic daring when the Tibetans woke up, the Gurkhas hot-footed it back to their camp, laughing their heads off like naughty schoolboys.

One bizarre tale is retold by the late John Masters, who served with the 4th Gurkha Regiment but is best known for his romantic novels about British India, notably *Bhowani Junction* of 1954, which is about the mixed-blood Anglo-Indians who served the British and was made into a film. Masters told of the Gurkhas' black humour when, at the cremation of one of their fellow soldiers, they saw to their astonishment that his corpse would not lie down. It kept sitting up in the flames, which gave the mourners a good laugh, and they continued to laugh uproariously when they leapt into the flames with their *kukris* and hacked the body to the ground, where it could be left in peace and make its burning exit from this world, as it was intended to do. Masters was clearly very impressed with his Gurkhas, and in the first part of his autobiography devoted pages in praise of their honour, courage and military prowess.

Most soldiers who have served with the Gurkhas talk of their self-belief and loyalty. Clearly, a soldier who keeps faith with himself and his fellow men, and goes cheerfully and steadfastly into combat without losing his nerve – however dangerous or apparently impossible the task – is an admirable and gutsy soldier, and if he happens to be very good indeed at the ugly business of killing, without surrendering to emotional sensitivity, so much the better. So it is not hard to see why a martial race such as the British thought so highly of Johnny Gurkha and were so unstinting in their praise. And if such a soldier has a good and enduring depth of spirit, that also is to his credit.

There can be no doubt that British and Gurkha soldiers have 'increased' one another and found the fellowship that they have needed by turning to their regiments and embracing one another's humanity and differences. They have done this in an amazing inter-racial spirit of goodwill that has drawn them together like magnets and made such a success of their partnership. It is this spirit that has attracted them as fellow travellers and brought out the best of their respective qualities.

It is certainly possible that Britain's first Gurkha soldiers did not think much of their own officers and commanders, according to the mixed-blood, Anglo-Indian military leader Captain Hyder Hearsey, who reported in August 1814, in *Historical Papers Relating to Kumaon*, that Gurkha commanders were 'ignorant, treacherous, faithless and avaricious to an extreme, after conquest and victory ... bloodthirsty and relentless, after defeat mean and abject'. But of the ordinary Gurkha soldier he said: 'They are hardy, endure privations and are very obedient, have not much distinction of caste, and are a neutral kind of Hindoo eating in mess almost everything they meet with, except beef. Under our government and officers they would make excellent soldiers, and numbers would on the event of a rupture join our standard, for the sake of 6 rupees per month, and form a proper Corps of Hill Rangers.'

In fact it was the Gurkhas' military commanders and rulers who ordered them to behead and cut off the noses and lips of their victims, and the British could be forgiven for thinking that their own superior and more civilised leadership and rule would allow them to prevail upon the Gurkha soldiers to desist from such inhumane barbarism. These were, after all, genial, courteous and generous men, when not plunging their wicked *kukris* into their foes.

When the Gurkhas took British prisoners, they did not, by all accounts, behead, savage or mutilate them, as they did others. On the contrary, they showed them the greatest respect and displayed a different side to their character.

No doubt, in the hierarchical Hindu scheme of things, the white-skinned, educated British could be held in higher esteem than the Untouchables and others lower down the ladder of mankind, because of who they were and how they had conducted themselves.

According to Shipp, the Gurkhas 'said we were not men, but devils, and that we must have descended from the skies.' And these devils were led by fifty-eight-year-old Colonel David Ochterlony, to whom a statue was erected in Calcutta. He was a remarkable fighting man and foremost among the first mixed-race Anglo-Indian fathers and military men to make a big name for themselves in India. It is estimated that he had thirteen wives of both Indian and Eurasian blood and it is a fact that he took his young Eurasian son with him on the Gurkha campaign. And, not being a racist, he had the approval of many Eurasians and Asians. Among the former he was a forerunner of the vibrant mixed-blood Anglo-Indian community, whose extraordinary and unparalleled fighting tradition remains alive and well in India to this day.

The Anglo-Indians, who won more 'Indian VCs' for military distinction and valour in India's three twentieth-century wars against Pakistan than any other Indian tribe, including the Gurkhas and Sikhs, have, since partition in 1947, emerged as a distinctive warrior class in their own right. But it is India they have served, rather than the British who originally spawned and trained them before proceeding to neglect them. Before partition, this new Anglo-Indian, or Indo-British, community included some very successful and high-profile people indeed, including Lord Roberts, who distinguished himself in the Kabul-to-Kandahar campaign of 1870 and was later supreme commander of the British forces in the Boer War (he was the grandson of a Rajput princess). Lord Liverpool, Britain's prime minister for nearly fifteen years during the early nineteenth century, had an Indian grandmother from Calcutta. Then, with his Hindu and Muslim wives, there was Sir William Fraser, whose Anglo-Indian children were brought up according to the religion of their mothers and each according to the occupation of the mother's family.

Another prominent Anglo-Indian was James Skinner, who founded Skinner's Horse (the famous 'Yellowboys', so called because of their colourful uniforms), the finest cavalry regiment in British India, which remains to this day second only in seniority to the Indian President's Sikh bodyguard in the Indian Army. Colonel Skinner was the half-caste son of a high-born Rajput mother and a Scottish military father, and the significance of his cavalry's yellow uniforms, chosen by Skinner himself, was that the yellow robes and the saffron face scarves were the colour of death, symbolising the pledge of all who rode with him that, unless they returned victorious from battle, they would rather die (indeed they were sworn to die rather than accept defeat). The motto of this cavalry regiment, which started life as the 1st Bengal Lancers and celebrates its bicentenary in 2003, was and remains 'The Bravery of Man – By the Help of God'.

The interbreeding of British soldiers with native Indian women in order to serve British military and other interests in India – and in order to have brown skins in amongst those natives, brown skins who were loyal to the British and would do their bidding – was how the Anglo-Indian race was born. And Skinner of Skinner's Horse was chief among those who were intended to exemplify this race at its best. So, as in the ethnic Gurkha regiments, Rajput warrior blood flowed through the regiment's veins from the outset.

To return to Ochterlony, in the Gurkhas' eyes he was the man of their dreams. After defeating them, he befriended them, offering them a sought-after place in the British Army that they admired so much. When the British finally emerged as victors, after the bloody carnage and struggle of 1814–16, the mutual admiration and respect that had developed between the adversaries quickly led to a bond that has endured for nearly two centuries. Under the terms of a peace treaty, the Gurkhas were invited to enlist as soldiers in the East India Company Army, fighting shoulder to shoulder with their British masters, as comrades in arms, as a result of which Nepal became what is often referred to as Britain's 'oldest ally' in Asia. To begin with, some 5,000 Gurkhas joined up straight away, only about half of whom were 'real Gurkhas' – that is, from the original tribes of the Gorkha kingdom.

Ochterlony can be compared to larger-than-life military figures today or in recent history – Norman Schwarzkopf of Gulf War fame, perhaps, or David Stirling, who founded the SAS. But so, too, can his old enemy, Prithvi Narayan Shah, who took his tiny Gorkha tribes to conquer the more powerful kingdoms of the Kathmandu valley to establish a kingdom of his own.

So it wasn't only Ochterlony who left his mark on history while doing very well for himself into the bargain. But it is true that, after the Governor-General of British India himself, the Anglo-Indian Ochterlony was the most prominent person, living in grand style in Delhi with his dozen or so wives.

When the British finally overthrew the army of the Gorkha kingdom, they paid tribute to its heroic leaders and 450 crack troops by letting them march proudly away, unharmed and into exile, with their arms and everything else intact. Until the

British arrived in west Nepal, the Gorkhas had fought and roundly defeated and massacred Asian soldiers, many (but not all) of whom turned and fled from their vicious opponents, so this martial race had long regarded themselves as invincible. But this invincibility lasted only until the British Army, after its initial defeat, taught them the lesson of a lifetime. In imparting this lesson, however, the British learnt a very hard lesson themselves, for these Gorkha adversaries had proved almost a match for their conquerors.

Many of the troops at the disposal of the British in India in the early days of Empire were, naturally enough, Indian irregulars or professionals rather than British, so it was the white British officers – skilfully leading and heroically fighting alongside their own men – who impressed the Gurkhas above all. And it was not long before the defeated Gurkhas were falling over themselves to join the British Army in droves. In a part of the world where the British East India Company Army was itself a mercenary force, reliant on soldiers of fortune, they were more than welcome. There was a great need for fighters such as the Gurkha of the Magar and Gurung. These Magar and Gurung Gurkhas were reportedly brought into the Indo-Nepalese caste, above the impure Untouchables, within a Hindu hierarchy that had no qualms about subjugating the Tibetan-Burman ethnic communities who got in its way.

The big thing that the Gurkhas learnt from – and liked about – the British was their discipline, and some of them managed to learn this before they enlisted with the British Indian Army, because two British deserters, Byrnes and Bell, had joined their ranks to teach them how to become a more disciplined force while they were still fighting against the British. Premble tells us that the two deserters also taught artillery, the English language, music and British marching tunes. He also records that in 1816 British troops were astonished when Nepalese soldiers entertained them with their own versions of such songs as 'The Soldier's Wife' and 'The Lass of Richmond Hill'. Clearly, the British fighting man had appealed to the imagination of Gurkha soldiers before the fall of the Gurkha dynasty and in consequence some of them were modelling themselves on the British in more ways than one.

It was this process of military and cultural assimilation in west Nepal that set the pattern for Johnny Gurkha's future in the British Army. He was regarded as a truly remarkable find – a template for the perfect soldier. A born killer, amenable to discipline, unquestioningly loyal, utterly dependable, heroic, not squeamish in the face of the blood and guts that must be spilt, and displaying a natural affection for his officers. What more could the British Army ask for?

Apart from the Sikhs – who had rebuffed him – and the British and their mixed-blood Anglo-Indians, who had eventually managed to defeat him (though at great cost), he was reckoned to stand head and shoulders above the rest.

But what were the Gurkhas themselves asking for in this relationship? Only time would tell. And while they might have been defeated, they would never be anything less than defiant. They were, after all, not British soldiers, and why should they fight for a cause other than their own? Why should they take the British cause as their own? How *could* they take to such a cause?

Yet the fact remains that they pledged themselves to the cause of their former enemy for eternity – or at least, to date, for the greater part of 200 years. The Gurkhas took orders in their own language from British officers who were required not only to learn Gurkhali but also to understand and respect Gurkha customs, traditions and methods.

If historians and other observers have been puzzled by the phenomenon of the Gurkhas joining the British Army in great numbers, one wouldn't think so from the monumental lack of comment. It seems to have been taken for granted that joining the British Army and staying with it until this day was the most natural and inevitable thing in the world for them to do, as if the British Army was their natural home from home.

Maybe it was. But maybe there has been a lack of insight among historians and the British military. Maybe the Gurkhas, like other soldiers before them, have been taken too much for granted. But how to account for the loyalty of the Gurkhas to the British in India, during the days of the Raj and thereafter, decade after decade? Why did Gurkha soldiers fight like tigers and put their lives on the line in order to save British necks in their touch-and-go wars against the formidable Sikhs in British India?

And why did the Gurkhas spring immediately to the defence of their British masters during the Indian Mutiny of 1857–8? At this critical time they could easily have tipped the balance of power against them, had they so wished, perhaps altering the course of history.

What was it about the British that appealed to the Gurkhas, and about the Gurkhas that caused them to identify with the

British cause? Why not an Asian rather than a British cause? And what did the Gurkhas really understand about foreign soldiers who might have come from the other side of the moon? Why should they care about them? What was going on in Gurkha heads and hearts?

These are the long-neglected questions of Gurkha military history with which this book will concern itself, as it considers the factual record. Perhaps they can be answered; perhaps not.

But the Cambridge University historian Kitson Clark is in no doubt that, unless we ask the kind of questions that 'are in the last resort unanswerable', then the 'problem and significance' of military battles and their effects on history 'cannot be defined'. He tells us this, in relation to the Battle of Waterloo, in his thought-provoking book *The Critical Historian*, and what he has to say about the need to understand the make-up of the men who fought at the Battle of Waterloo applies no less to the role of the Gurkhas in the many historically significant battles they fought in the service of the British.

The question in these pages is not merely what makes a larger-than-life fighting man but what makes a larger-than-life Gurkha fighting man and why did he choose to fight for Britain in so many wars around the world? The factual record – written almost entirely by soldiers – does not, in fact, speak for itself in this matter. It speaks of military matters in military terms.

Clark also says: 'But to consider such questions in order to try to estimate what may have been the result of men's actions, as also to guess what is happening in their thoughts, requires qualities of mind which a mere knowledge of the facts can never give. Indeed the imagination and insight which can enlighten these problems could do so even when knowledge of the facts is less complete than it could be or when liberties have been taken with the facts. That is why an old-fashioned history written by a man of insight and genius can be of more value than a modern one written by a pedant and heavy with the results of the most recent research. That is, also, why an historical novelist can sometimes give an insight into the past which many historians, who stick to the fenced pathway of what is probable and accurate, cannot give. Nevertheless it is very dangerous to neglect or to tamper with any part of the framework of fact. The facts are the only part of history about which there is any degree of certainty; all interpretation, all reconstruction, is speculative, and if it does not respect the facts, speculation is certainly worthless and may be deceptive.'

When looking into the factual framework of the Gurkhas' story, one cannot fail to respect that history. But if we are to get at the man behind the facts – behind the image – then there is a need for imaginative insight of the kind referred to by Clark.

We are told by observers who have fought with and against the Gurkhas that they are cheerful, jolly and good-humoured, courteous and generous, and, at the same time, savage and cruel. This is a striking and deeply curious contradiction. We also learn, from John Shipp's memoirs, of the amazing contrasts in the landscape from which the Gurkhas come – beautiful yet cold, with dreary glens where tigers prowl, though not as savage as the flinty-hearted Gurkhas who practise their ugly arts of war in among their flinty rocks. Perhaps there is a clue here that helps to explain the contradictory nature of the Gurkha people and how it has been shaped by their environment. On the one hand, there is enough beauty in the Nepalese landscape to lift and cleanse the human spirit and imprint it with profound kindliness and romance. But there is also the harshest poverty and discomfort in the hill villages to blight the most generous, friendly and romantic souls and break all but the strongest hearts. And in such an unrelenting landscape, people must, in order to survive, harden their hearts and become at least as hard and unyielding as the cruel natural environment in which they find themselves.

Perhaps there is a symmetry between the contradictory and unyielding landscape and the contradictory and unyielding race it produces. Of course, this is only a theory, but I believe that it is imaginative speculation of this kind that might help us to understand the paradox of the Gurkha temperament – beauty and cruelty, gentleness and savagery, spirituality and brutality, all are hallmarks of the Nepalese landscape. Whilst these opposites manifest themselves in all races, they do so most noticeably in the Gurkha race.

In the meantime, on with our story. From here on, the British East India Company and Nepal kept out of each other's way, while the former got on with the business of wrapping up India and its lucrative markets.

Even so, the political relationship remained sensitive. This was highlighted by an occurrence early in the twentieth century after the British had allowed some Gurkhas to become officers in their Indian Army, where they could order and lead their own men. Known as the Viceroy's Commissioned

Officers (VCOs), they were not fully commissioned officers of the King of England and were ranked below British officers. A number of VCOs were invited to attend King Edward VII on ceremonial duties in Britain for three months, under a scheme he had introduced in order to honour Britain's native VCOs in India – not just Gurkhas but all native officers – and doubtless to show them off to unaccustomed British eyes.

Rudyard Kipling wrote a true short story, 'In the Presence', about four Gurkha officers who went to England to mount a guard at Edward VII's lying-in-state in 1910. Whereas British Grenadier Guards stood for only half an hour since there were many more of them to relieve one another, each Gurkha stood with head bowed for an hour while the other three took a break for three hours. In addition, they had to wear higher collars than those to which they were accustomed, and these cut into their short necks. And, to add insult to injury, they had no opportunity to prepare their own food, so had to live on uncooked grain, washed down with water, because their religion forbade them to eat English food. (Had they eaten it they could have been excommunicated from their caste.) All in all, they weren't happy.

When the time came for three of the four Gurkhas to deliver a wreath to the deceased king – whom they called Wanidza, for Windsor – the luckless fourth officer's stamina was stretched to the limit because there was no one to relieve him for four hours. Yet these Gurkhas did the disciplined and honourable thing and endured all this without complaint and with the greatest patience, politeness, fortitude and loyalty. This is the point of Kipling's story, which tells us: 'And so it was done

– not in hot blood, not for a little while, not yet with the smell of slaughter to sustain, but in silence, for a very long time, rooted to one place, before the Presence, among the most terrible feet of the multitude.' Kipling makes a big thing about the endless procession of mourners – a 'river of feet' that made the Gurkhas' vigil such a long drawn-out affair – and the fact that, with their heads bowed, they could see only the mourners' feet, and could not look them in the eye. On this occasion it was, for a change, Gurkha honour off the battlefield that was being portrayed, but the event was to raise questions of the wider implications for their honour back home in Nepal and for their regiment in India.

What happened was that after the real-life 'honoured' Gurkhas returned to India and one of them, Santbir Gurung, went back to Nepal in 1913, he was excommunicated from his religion and banished from his country, because he had forgotten to ask Maharaja Chandra Shamsher's permission to accept the King of England's invitation. So, having been honoured in England, he found himself dishonoured in his own country and forced into exile. Chandra Shamsher had been on a tiger hunt with George V (who had visited Nepal as the Prince of Wales before he became king), but he would not budge for the king when he intervened on behalf of the dishonoured Gurkha officer. Gurung's applications to be allowed back into his country and return to his religion were repeatedly rejected over many years, until after the Maharaja's death in 1938. By now eighty-three, he underwent a re-purification ceremony to be readmitted to his caste and country so that he would not die an outcast.

So the situation remained delicate between Britain and Nepal, and Gurkha officers were, alas, withdrawn from King Edward VII's scheme.

The sympathies of King George V were with Santbir Gurung, to whom he sent a portrait of his father, inscribed with the words 'In memory of your vigil'. His vigil was for security rather than religious purposes. In their long relationship with the British, the Gurkhas have performed many extraordinary vigils on and off the field of battle and this book, like King George V's message, is in memory of them. It is in memory of men whose 'harsh lives', as C.J. Stranks has observed in his introduction to Shipp's memoirs, 'made the hardships of army life a little less killing for them than they were for others'; who had 'the habit of victory and should they happen to be beaten showed as much surprise as chagrin at the result; and who lived in 'a world in which hardness was the price of survival, and unchecked pity a burden which few could bear'.

Stranks says that, looking back on British India now, 'we can see what an astonishing thing it was for a few men, from a distant island, dependent on slow and uncertain communications, to spread over a whole sub-continent and in the end dominate it... Shipp ... tells us what it was like to march and fight for thirty-six hours on end, without sleep, on an empty belly, of the men's reckless courage, of their jokes of what it meant to be left behind wounded on the battlefield... All this going on in the torrential rains or searing heat of India.'

Astonishment is right. Back in Britain – and gradually in the world at large – people were going to be amazed by events in

India, by the wondrous potential of it all, the rich and fascinating tapestry that would unfold there. And this is why so many people and different countries wanted a slice of the action, and why Britain was so determined to keep those incredible riches all to itself.

But India would be a tremendous and hard-fought struggle, and one in which the Gurkhas were quickly recognised as having a crucial part to play, not only in the enormous challenge of conquering the Indian sub-continent, but in the policing of it afterwards. The British had the imagination to see what India could become, just as – when there remained no doubt that they had overstayed their welcome – they had the imagination to go home (unlike the Muslim invaders before them, who stayed on and remain unwanted to this day).

And the British also had the imagination to envisage a military role for Johnny Gurkha in the overall scheme of things.

India was the making of Johnny Gurkha and, without it, there was not much chance of an immediate or long-term future for him, either on his own account in that part of the world, or in the service of the British, not only in India but in many other parts of the world as well.

## three

# FACE TO FACE WITH THE PATHANS

As we have seen, it was not long after the Gurkhas clashed with the British on the bloody battlefields of west Nepal that they found themselves marching into a new destiny in India alongside their former enemies.

At the political level it was a marriage of convenience, with Nepal supplying cheap military manpower in return for British cash and the promise of no further incursions or interference. But on the personal level the alliance between Gurkha soldiers and their British officers was less calculating, more sincere, as trust and comradeship rapidly developed.

The British military trusted its Gurkhas not to let it down during the Indian Mutiny and it was not disappointed. Not only did Gurkhas come to the rescue of the British, but they even broke a Hindu taboo by executing their own kind in Meerut in 1857, shooting Brahmin soldiers who were among the first of the mutineers. Only once had a Gurkha regiment mutinied against the Brits, and that was on a very small scale. In Almora, the 3rd Gurkhas took great exception to a proposed reduction in their already paltry pay and expenses, but the matter was swiftly sorted out by the British, who conceded that the Gurkhas had a point, and removed their own Commanding Officer.

India was no easy ride for the Gurkhas – any more than it was for the British – yet they stuck it out bravely and with distinction on behalf of the invaders, whom they served loyally. In fact India was one of the world's toughest theatres of war, a hard training ground for the resolution of military problems, not only in the sub-continent, but also in British battles elsewhere around the globe. It was a handy place for the Gurkhas and others to cut their teeth in the service of the British, practising the kind of warfare that would stand them in good stead later on in combat elsewhere.

Mention has already been made of the traditional Gurkha propensity for severing heads and, once upon a distant time, noses and lips as well, but their horrifying talents in this respect were as nothing compared with those of the infamous Pathans, a murderous and fanatical Muslim tribe from Afghanistan and what is now Pakistan, who were waiting for them in British India with a bloodlust all their own.

Not that the impassive Gurkhas were likely to lose much sleep about this, for supposedly they did not scare easily or at all – or, if they did, they took life and its innumerable fears fatalistically, as their religion taught. In fact they had already shown that they did not seem to have the usual anguish that soldiers of many other races experienced when exposed for the first time to the atrocious carnage of battle.

There had never been any signs of the Gurkhas being revolted by blood and guts, so they were expected to have cast-iron stomachs and, as far as the hostile Afghans and Pathans were concerned, the 5th Gurkha Regiment soon distinguished itself on the notorious North-West Frontier, where it became known as the 'frontier force' of India. During the Second Afghan War, of 1878–80, the 5th Gurkhas, in the company of British troops, repulsed no fewer than 18,000 tribal Afghan warriors. With seven VCs to its merit, and the prefix 'Royal' added to its name for the impressive way it policed the border, it became the premier Gurkha regiment of the elite Gurkha Brigade in India, which Prime Minister Pandit Nehru took care to keep after partition in 1947.

British soldiers and their accomplices who fell foul of the Pathans could expect to be beheaded and/or castrated, the latter not infrequently carried out by a Muslim woman who entertained herself in this way and might also choke and drown her victims to death by urinating into their mouths.

Pathans – and Waziris – thought nothing of flogging their defenceless prisoners to death, before chopping off the penis and testicles, perhaps popping them into the soldiers' mouths, and then skinning their bodies for good measure, making sure to peg out their skins on rocks for all to see. They thought nothing of cutting their victims' private parts to ribbons and ripping open their stomachs. This fate was not an uncommon one for some of the British military in India in those days.

And certainly it awaited the Gurkhas, Sikhs, mixed-race Anglo-Indians and others who enlisted in the service of the British. The Gurkhas soon found themselves in hand-to-hand fighting with Pathans and Waziris, both of whom had heard about the Gurkhas and were itching to test themselves against them. But, as usual, the Gurkhas and their British officers did not flinch as they bayoneted and *kukri*-ed their foes to death, sometimes giving the tribesmen a dose of their own savage and revolting medicine where mutilation was concerned.

Often, when Afghanistan is mentioned these days, much is made of one of the worst defeats to be suffered by the British anywhere in Asia. This occurred in 1880, just outside Kandahar, at the hands of Ayub Khan and his 20,000 tribal Afghan warriors, among them a great many ferocious Pathans. This defeat, which has stuck to Britain's military reputation ever since, is usually mentioned on television news programmes in the new millennium as an example of how unconquerable the fearless Afghans have always been. It is mentioned by newscasters and journalists who really should check their history.

On the contrary, Afghans and Pathans have not always been invincible. That terrible but single defeat happened when Brigadier-General George Burrows seriously and stupidly underestimated the strength of the enemy, and decided to take them on, only to find himself hopelessly outnumbered and seriously outgunned. This was an atrocious and lamentable tactical blunder for which the British were to pay a high price. Burrows's 2,500 force was butchered virtually to extinction. Commentators focus on this aspect nowadays, but almost never is it said how bravely his soldiers fought against such overwhelming and unfair odds, or how they killed five times as many of their enemy as Pathans and others killed them, or how swiftly the British Army in India revenged itself, ruthlessly massacring Pathans and other Afghan tribal warriors in a follow-up battle conducted by Lord Roberts, who made it quite clear to the enemy who was boss.

In those wild times many British officers and soldiers regarded themselves as 'half Pathan' when it came to hand-to-hand fighting, which they entered into with an absolute relish, and Gurkhas had to become half Pathan likewise. Queuing up on the North-West Frontier to prove themselves against Pathans and other tribesmen, they looked forward to taking on the ferocious tribesmen and defeating them. This is how Burrows came to make his fatal mistake. He reckoned that there could not be that many Afghans marching with Ayub Khan, and in any case he didn't seem to care very much if the odds were just a little against his men, since this would simply allow them to demonstrate their superiority by defeating the enemy in such circumstances. The glory-seeking British were never looking for an easy fight against feeble opposition. It really mattered to them that they should prove themselves to be the world's best soldiers, fairly and squarely. Today this seems hard to understand or even to believe, but that's how British soldiers and their Gurkha partners thought and behaved in battle in those distant times, and this appealed equally to Afghan and Pathan tribesmen, who also enjoyed the sport of war and admired the British for their outstanding fighting abilities.

The grooming of the Gurkhas by the British for their role in the Indian sub-continent and subsequently on the world military stage coincided with the so-called 'Great Game'. Played by the Western powers, this was a protracted struggle for the exploitation and colonisation of the sub-continent, which was regarded as a magnificent jewel for anybody's crown, and the Russian Bear in particular was sniffing around the northern frontiers of India and Afghanistan, as it still does to this day.

In his book *The Great Game*, Peter Hopkirk tells us: 'Outnumbered, outmanoeuvred and outgunned, and tormented by heat and thirst, the British and Indian troops nonetheless fought magnificently. Much of the fighting was hand-to-hand. Afghans were pulled onto British bayonets by their beards, while other attacks were beaten off with rocks as ammunition ran low. Finally the order was given for a fighting withdrawal to Kandahar under cover of darkness. By the time the shattered remnants of the force reached Kandahar to break the appalling news to the garrison there, Burrows had lost nearly a thousand of his men, even if they had left nearly five times that number of the enemy dead or dying on the plain... Having buried his own dead (leaving the British corpses to the vultures), Ayub Khan now turned his attention to the capture of Kandahar. Immediately, the garrison prepared to face a siege. For a start, because of the risk of treachery from within, it was decided to take the drastic step of expelling from the city all male Afghans of fighting age. More than 12,000 were ordered out, many at gunpoint, by the 3,000 defenders. The first anyone in India knew of the disaster was when the telegraph operator at Simla received an urgent, clear-the-line signal. Moments later came the grim tidings from Kandahar. "Total defeat and dispersion of General Burrows's force. Heavy loss in both officers and men." The final death toll was not yet known, the message added, as small groups of survivors were still coming in.'

Those who were left of a mere 3,000 men – after an original British force of 4,000 had reduced Ayub Khan's 20,000 to 15,000 – were small groups for sure. The battle of Rorke's Drift in Natal in 1879, where the British fought against overwhelming numbers of Zulus, is in the same league for bravery against such overwhelming odds as this. But there are no such films to remind us of this battle with Ayub Khan.

After Ayub Khan's massacre of the British, Hopkirk writes, 'it was decided to dispatch him [General Roberts] at once at the head of a 10,000 strong force to destroy Ayub Khan's army and relieve Kandahar. The 300 mile forced march was expected to take him a month, for all supplies had to be carried, and the route lay across harsh and hostile territory. In fact, it was one of the most rapid marches in military history. The entire force, including infantry, cavalry, light artillery, field hospitals, ammunition and even mutton on the hoof, reached the beleaguered city in twenty days. On hearing that the greatly feared Roberts was on his way to avenge the British defeat, Ayub Khan took fright and withdrew from his positions around Kandahar. He even sent a message to Roberts insisting that the British had forced him to do battle with them ... asking the general how matters could best be resolved between himself and the British, with whom he insisted he wanted to be friends. But Roberts was in no mood for such dalliance... the two sides were evenly matched, although the Afghans enjoyed considerable superiority in artillery. At first Ayub Khan's troops resisted ferociously, pouring down a heavy fire on the advancing British. Soon, however, the bayonets of the 72nd Highlanders and the *kukris* of the 2nd Gurkhas began to tell. By lunchtime all the Afghan artillery was in Roberts's hands, and as darkness fell, the battle was over. British losses totalled only 35 dead, while the Afghans left more than 600 corpses on the battlefield, taking as many others with them as they fled. Although weakened by illness, Roberts had commanded the entire operation from the saddle, taking occasional sips of champagne to keep up his strength. With Britain's military prestige in Central Asia now restored ... and with a strong and friendly ruler on the throne in Kabul ... [the British] Cabinet decided to offer Kandahar to Abdur Rahman on the grounds that the less the British interfered in the affairs of Afghanistan, the less hostility there would be towards then, and the more inclined the Afghans would be to resist the Russians as they previously had the British.'

There is no question that the British quickly retrieved the situation in Afghanistan, where they thoroughly defeated the Pathans and other tribal warriors. But, after vanquishing this enemy, they had bigger fish to fry elsewhere in the sub-continent, and it would have stretched them too much to have had to hold Afghanistan, the only conceivable interest of which to them, in those empire-building days, was as a buffer state against the Russians, whom they were determined to keep out of India at all costs. As for Afghan and Pathan warriors, they held no overwhelming fear for British, Gurkha or other Indian troops, who beat them on the battlefield not once but several times (Roberts had won a significant victory once before and there would be more encounters to follow, although both times with Roberts, the British, of course, suffered heavy losses). While the British always respected Afghan and Pathan warriors, they did not regard them as invincible – too much trouble, maybe, but not invincible.

Hopkirk also recounts that when 'Colonel William Dennie, a soldier of legendary bravery', stormed Ghazni, 'the Afghans, who had never dreamed that their stronghold could be stormed, fought back with the utmost courage and ferocity. But it was the first time they had encountered highly trained European troops well versed in modern siege tactics, and soon the defence began to crumble... the Afghans rushed out from their hiding places, sword in hand ... but only to meet with fearful retribution from the musket-fire of the British infantry... Some were bayoneted on the ground. Others were pursued and hunted into corners like mad dogs and shot down... Those who managed to escape through the gateway or over the wall were cut down by the cavalry outside. Soon it was all over, and the Union Jack and regimental standards of the assault parties fluttered in triumph from the ramparts. It was an overwhelming victory for the British, as the casualty figures showed. They had lost only 17 dead, with a further 165 wounded, 18 of them officers. At least 500 of the defenders had died during the fighting within the fortress, while many others had been cut down outside... The way was clear to the Afghan capital, less than a hundred miles to the north... The sudden and unexpected loss of Ghazni proved a devastating blow to Dost Mohammed. A 5,000-strong Afghan cavalry force commanded by his son, which had been sent to try to halt the advancing British, turned back rather than face annihilation... The British appeared before the walls of Kabul. Dost Mohammed, they found, had fled, and the capital surrendered without a shot being fired... In the meantime, in Kabul, the British settled down to the daily routine of garrison life. Race-meetings were organised, business flourished in the bazaars as the British and Indian troops spent their earnings there.'

The Gurkhas were always up to their ears in trouble as they fought alongside the British in India and Afghanistan, and together with the Sikhs, mixed-race Anglo-Indians and others, they were often caught in the crossfire between the British and the various factions throughout the sub-continent with whom their imperialist masters waged war. India at this time was one giddy round of slaughter.

The Sikhs eventually joined the British, but they resisted the idea at first, and during the first of the two Sikh Wars in the Punjab, they fought against the invading British and the Gurkhas, a campaign in which once again the Gurkhas won the admiration of the colonial power. While it was the policy of the British, as far as possible, to keep the Gurkhas away from the Indians, confining them instead to remote border areas where they could usefully deter any invaders and keep a watchful eye on warring tribesmen, the British were in no doubt that they needed Gurkha assistance against the near-invincible Sikhs. So they sent in the Nasiri and Sirmoor battalions. And the Gurkhas certainly rose to the challenge, as recorded at the time by General Sir Hugh Grant, who reportedly said: 'The determined hardihood and bravery with which our two battalions of Goorkhas ... met the Sikhs wherever they opposed them. Soldiers of small stature and indomitable spirit, they vied in ardent courage in the charge with the Grenadiers of our own nation and armed with the short weapon of the mountains were a terror to the Sikhs throughout the whole combat.'

To be a terror to the Sikhs is no small achievement, but when the British eventually managed to defeat the Sikhs, the latter then took a leaf out of Johnny Gurkha's book and joined the British Indian Army, no doubt to everyone's relief.

A good number of Pathans and others would do the same in due course. And to be a terror to the Pathans was something else. With regard to the Pathans in Afghanistan and along the North West Frontier today, not much appears to have changed since that time, except that the natives are better armed and the borders are no longer heavily manned by Gurkha regiments, as once they were. Crushing the menace of the Pathans was no easy task for the Gurkhas, to whom these tribesmen, though weird and horrifying to the British, were no mystery in this betwixt-and-between-place, part India and part Central Asia. There is no doubt that British soldiers would have had a much harder time of it without Gurkha assistance in the terrain of the North-West Frontier. The region was characterised by its snow and sleet that fell in thick flurries and was blown about so gustily that soldiers, horses and guns were not always clearly or at all visible. Against this weird, dreamlike canvas, bloodthirsty Pathan tribesmen, clouded by snow, suddenly came at the British and their Gurkha troops like terrifying white ghosts, with a deadly fleetness of frozen foot. As the wild geese from Tibet flew south, the thunder of their wings echoing overhead, the running Pathan knifemen fell upon the enemy like a torrent of spiteful hailstones in their white-hot fury.

In naked contrast to the rest of India – with the suffocating heat and dust of its teeming millions, its grey, gritty soil and scrub and stunted trees in desert regions, its heatstroke-inducing trains, its tiger's breath on your cheek in dark-green jungle settings, its bullock carts, camels, barking dogs and snake charmers, its wildly colourful regimental splendour, its Maharajas' palaces and durbars, its moonlight under the mango trees – the North-West Frontier was a hard, cold and grim place to be spilling blood at 18 degrees above zero; red blood running freely through a deathly white landscape in which only the most determined to survive in hand-to-hand fighting could expect to reach middle age. On both sides, young heads rolled as the British Gurkha regiments slowly got the better of the Pathans, to the echo of silver trumpets and the crack of gunshot, the flash and glint of steel, the spine-curdling shrieks, the usual agonising deathly groans and croaks of men lost in battle. With the clink-clank of scabbard and *kukri* ringing in the combatants' ears, cold-blue British and dark-brown Gurkha eyes burnt together in the heat of battle in a furious vision of horror that met with black Pathan eyes that were as much terrified by their enemies' eyes as were their enemies by theirs. As the Gurkhas chewed cardamom seeds to steady their nerves and sweeten the crawling smell of death, and as the strong, gathering smell of their sweat mixed with the fresh smell of the cardamom and their own and their enemies' fresh blood, they fought with rifles, bayonets, *kukris*, stones, boots and fists, as we learn from John Masters.

This was also the country of Rudyard Kipling's story 'The Man Who Would Be King', on which was based the 1975 film of that title starring Michael Caine, Sean Connery and Christopher Plummer.

This was Kipling's 'eagles is screamin' around us' country, with its 'river's a-moaning below/We're clear o' the pine an' the oak-scrub, we're out on the rocks an' the snow/An' the wind is as thin as the whip-lash what carries away to the plains/The rattle an' stamp of the lead mules, the jinglety-jink o' the chains.'

It was in this extremely dangerous and hostile terrain that Gurkha soldiers and their British officers trudged through the snow to fight Pathans and police the borders. A visit to the Gurkha Museum in Winchester brings alive the battles against the Pathans in no uncertain way. Visitors are led through a Gurkha military history that features very realistic life-size models of soldiers and battles from different countries and eras. In the North-West Frontier section, which recalls the days when the Gurkhas policed the border there for the British Raj, visitors enter a dark and silent room that suddenly comes alive as soon as the first footstep in Pathan territory triggers an alarm (carefully concealed, presumably, under the floor covering). A loud and frightening war cry of '*Allah Akhbar*' ('God is great') suddenly hits visitors, right out of the darkness and silence, the lights come on and visitors are dramatically confronted (top marks to the Gurkha Museum) by a model of a ferocious Pathan glaring in their direction and shouting 'Death to the infidel', coming at them with his dagger. The simulation is unnerving and utterly convincing. The museum's historical Pathans from past times look remarkably similar to the Pashtuns we have seen recently in television reports from Afghanistan. It is well worth a visit to Winchester to see this museum. If it were on the tourist route in London, it would be playing to packed houses.

Oddly enough, Muslim Pathans and Afghans of the North-West Frontier claim to be of Jewish descent. This is explained in a museum fact sheet about the Frontier: 'The Afghan proper, that is to say, the Durani clans, call themselves the Ben-i-Israel, the Children of Israel, and the legendary ancestor is one Kais, the chief of the descendants of a Jewish settlement in the Mountains of Ghor, which lie north-west of Kandahar, and which to this day have never been visited by Europeans. To one of the three sons of Kais, all Afghan and Pathan tribes trace their origin, and cling to the Jewish legend. Kais was said to be thirty-seventh in descent from Saul, and lived in the days of the Prophet. There are settlements of professing Jews in Bokhara who preserve what may be an original legend... the Afghans hold strongly by their Jewish origin, and their names, Jacob and Joseph and Isaac and Abraham and the like, do not belie the tale... All Pathans speak Pukhtu or Pushtu... The country of the Pathans is much of it craggy and inhospitable, freezing in winter and scorching in summer. It has been called a gigantic slag-heap. It will barely support human life at the simplest level and the Pathan must get the price of a wife or a rifle from somewhere else, whether by force or fraud, by raiding or trading, or simply by blackmail – such as a subsidy from the government in the plains.'

It was this subsidy that the Pathans got from the British in India and it was their brute force and raiding that the Gurkhas helped the British to contain along the border. There was a lot of territory to police, but it is widely agreed that the Gurkhas and their British officers did it remarkably well. It would be wrong to suggest, though, that the Gurkhas were the only crack force on the North-West Frontier – or anywhere else in India, for that matter. There were many brave and heroic soldiers who were not Gurkhas who did a very good job of holding the frontier. And some of them were as wild and ferocious as any Pathan, whose Pukhtunwali code of custom and honour confers on him, according to the Gurkha Museum, 'certain rights and requires of him certain duties. The most important of the duties is badal, vengeance; he *must* exact vengeance, at any risk and at all cost, for an insult or injury done to himself, his family, his clan or his tribe. If he dies, then they must take up the quarrel…The Pathan may wait for years for his chance, but take it he must, sooner or later, or be utterly shamed…The people are as craggy as the country, unswerving in the most fundamental forms of Islam, bitter in the blood-feud, reckless in life… Since a Pathan's survival depended on shooting first… principles of fair play, came low, in the scale of virtues… Having nothing else to do with their time, they would study for days or weeks the habits of a convoy-escort, a standing piquet … until they saw develop some careless habit or tactical error… All the same, it is wrong to think of the Frontier as an unrelieved study in barbarism. The tribesmen looked on war as an honourable, exciting, and manly exercise. When they had no quarrel with the British or the Afghans they arranged one among themselves. Many of them clearly thought the [British] Government of India organized the Frontier wars on the same basis… Many [Pathans] were characters, some could be described as 'cards'… Do not let a man [Pathan] approach you in enemy country scratching his stomach, he is looking for his knife. Hit him on the elbow with a stick and he'll drop it… Avoid shaking hands with strange Pathans. They will seize with their left hand and stab with their right on occasions… there was among middle-rank and junior [British] officers a feeling … that if the Frontier was always at peace, India would be a much duller place … that the army benefited immeasurably from annual war-games with the best umpire in the world, who never let a mistake go unpunished.'

# four

# THE GURKHAS IN CENTRAL ASIA

It was across the North-West Frontier that Johnny Gurkha first made the acquaintance of Britain's last imperial explorer, the legendary adventurer and mystic Sir Francis Younghusband, who has been compared for his exploits in Central Asia to the likes of Marco Polo, General Charles Gordon ('Chinese Gordon') and Lawrence of Arabia (T.E. Lawrence).

It was a young captain Younghusband who was given an escort of six Gurkha soldiers for a mission to protect British interests when the Russians started to raise the tempo of the Great Game on the Frontier, where they were attempting to do deals with various tribes, including the Hunza.

Under the leadership of the celebrated and formidable Colonel Grombtchevski, the Russians were becoming a thorn in British flesh, so Younghusband was sent into highly dangerous Hunza territory to put a stop to it. His mission was to discover a secret pass used by Hunza raiders and to find out what Grombtchevski was up to, so that, when the time came, the British would know precisely where and how best to invade the Hunza kingdom.

When told by local tribesmen, who were terrorised by the Hunza, that the first man to enter Hunza territory would definitely be killed, Younghusband is reputed to have turned to his Gurkha corporal and wise-cracked that he should go first! Whereupon the corporal is supposed to have beamed with satisfaction at the prospect (unless he was just enjoying the joke). But, little touches like this show up in a flash the characteristics of different races, and not least the Gurkha characteristic of facing adversity and danger with a good sense of humour and a smile on one's face.

It was thanks in no small part to the Gurkhas that the first British officer was going into Hunza and other Central Asian territories for the first time. Younghusband's dangerous mission was to locate the Mir of Hunza, a notorious Central Asian slave trader and tribal ruler, and to give him a piece of the British government's mind. It was also to encounter Grombtchevski, who was great bear of a man with a thick black beard. But Grombtchevski was not unfriendly. He invited Younghusband to dinner, at which the host was escorted by his Cossack soldiers, of whom the Gurkhas were apparently dismissive, thinking them not very well disciplined and also very poorly equipped.

The meeting with Grombtchevski was another first for the Gurkhas – the first encounter between deadly rivals in the Great Game – what a story Kipling could have made of this –

whilst also being the first British soldiers into Central Asia. We are told that, when Younghusband said goodbye to Grombtchevski, the Russian was witty enough to tell him that he hoped that they might meet again, either in peace or at war, and that in either case Younghusband would be sure of a warm welcome!

It is a pity that such civilised wits were, in those times, destined to spill each other's blood. But, if this Russian bear was indeed an excellent wit, as things turned out the last laugh was on him, when his Cossacks caught frostbite and their ponies died, as a result of which Grombtchevski almost didn't get back to Russia, where he arrived a year late and on crutches.

The Mir of Hunza was reckoned to be a nasty piece of work. Brutal and heartless, he had reportedly poisoned his own father and thrown two of his brothers over a precipice. He was, by all accounts, unpredictable and not infrequently off his head, so Younghusband and his Gurkhas knew they had better keep their wits about them, and not lose their nerve, if they wanted to live to tell the tale. One can well imagine how these brave gladiators must have felt when they stepped into the lion's den! As for the Mir, goodness knows what he might have been feeling, but he must at least have been impressed with their apparent lack of fear. Perhaps he was puzzled, or maybe even flattered that they had risked their skins to pay him such an unexpected and unheard of visit. He had good reason to be wary.

When they decided to entertain him with a show of strength – by firing their rifles in quick succession – he challenged them to prove their accuracy by shooting at one of his men on the far side of the valley to see if they could hit him. It seems that they declined the offer, in which case he doubtless thought them rather nesh. But the Mir was, by all accounts, impressed with Younghusband and his Gurkhas, so no harm came to them and they parted amicably, the British having pin-pointed exactly where he was and the secret route by which he and his kingdom could be accessed and overthrown. But what a sigh of relief they must have taken when they marched out of Hunza. It must have been like a handful of men marching out of Hitler's Germany, Stalin's Russia, or Genghis Khan's Mongol empire without having come to harm.

When Younghusband invaded Tibet, the Gurkhas were to the fore again. The weather, so high up in the mountains, was colder still. Coming from that part of the world – Tibet borders on Nepal and is today an administrative region of Western China – the Gurkhas were ideal running mates for Younghusband. They were well used to fighting to the death, and fighting uphill on steep mountain and valley slopes, under falling rocks and on slippery and exposed rocky terrain, where there was not much cover to which one could run. Tibet consists of a monumentally high plateau that is surrounded by mountains, so it is a difficult nut to crack for those on the outside, with invasion in mind, and who must foot-slog it all the way in bitterly cold weather, dragging their heavy equipment, arms and supplies with them. Of course, Tibet is easier to access from China, which is on the right side of the mountains, with convenient access to the interior of the country, and this is doubtless why the Chinese have been able to have their way in the country since the 1950s, where they have brutally suppressed the people. It is a mineral-rich country of river valleys and nomads and Buddhist priests who have had a continuing and profound influence on Tibetans since the 7th century AD. But when the British first went there, it was a mystery to the outside world, particularly the Western and European worlds, and even the Indians were not overly familiar with the place in those days. The Indians were not unaware of its existence, since it bordered on India and Burma, as well as Nepal, and included the Himalayas among its surrounding mountains. But, until they joined the ranks of the British army, Indians did not generally have reason to go there, and who could blame them?

But to the British, Tibet really was the other side of the moon.

It was Younghusband who made a treaty with the Dalai Lama and opened up Tibet to Western trade, and he did this with the invaluable help of the Gurkhas. He also explored Manchuria in 1886 and discovered the route from Kashgar into India via the Mustagh Pass. The discovery of inland passes and routes into mysterious and secret places – in the days before aeroplanes, cable cars, iron bridges, railways, motorways, motorised vehicles, tanks and armoured cars – was all important to sturdy and determined empire builders and world traders such as the British, whose soldiers and explorers had so often to walk, climb, march and fight their way into inaccessible territories, over many hundreds and thousands of miles, every inch of the way. It was of benefit to Indian traders also.

The first reliable motorcars – with a top speed of 18 miles per hour! – did not find their way on to European roads until 1898, four years before Younghusband's treaty in Tibet, and the only so-called 'modern' motorcycles that there were, had not hit European roads until 1860 (not that either of these vehicles would have been of any use in Central Asia's rocky terrain).

There were ships, of course – and the English had built the world's first all-iron, propeller-driven steam ship (called the *Great Britain* and designed by Brunel in 1843), which took fifteen days to cross the Atlantic to New York – but they were of no use inland.

One of the most useful weapons of empire building – apart from a pair of sturdy legs and arms on the body of a gusty soldier – was, in addition to fire power and the sword, the bayonet, which had been in use since the 17$^{th}$ century when it replaced the pike at a place called Bayonne in South West France. This is because so much of the fighting was hand-to-hand. Whilst horses and canon were no less useful, they could not always be used in difficult terrain, and the sword was not much of an accompaniment to a rifle, although it was very effective in a cavalry charge. The earliest bayonets were jammed into the barrel of a gun, which could not then be fired, and this was a very definite drawback that was not resolved until the 1680s when some bright spark thought of attaching a socket to a tube and slipping this over the muzzle, so that the musket or rifle could still be fired while the bayonet was also in action (early muskets had daggers rather than bayonets hooked onto their muzzles). Not exactly rocket science this, but it made all the difference to the effectiveness of the bayonet, which is what the British showed to the Gurkhas when they first met them in Western Nepal on the field of battle, and when they became familiar, by return, with the Gurkha *kukri*.

It is against this fascinating technological and machine-age background that one can better appreciate the impressive nature and significance of the hard fought achievements of Younghusband and others as they marched out into the world with their Gurkha and other soldiers, rifles firing and bayonets at the ready.

And it was an excursion to the Roof of the World in Tibet that resulted in Gurkha, Sikh, Indian and British soldiers going into combat against the Tibetans at 18,500 feet, to win the highest skirmish ever to be fought in military history, defeating their foe after three hours of fighting, and setting their eyes for the first time on the Dalai Lama's 1,000-room winter palace, with its golden roof. It was yet another first for the Gurkhas. This time the highest skirmish above sea level to be fought in military history, to add to the achievement of escorting the first British officer to enter a notorious no-go area in Central Asia and then being there to witness the first time that rivals in the Great Game met face to face – with little Johnny Gurkha as referee, as it were, between the Russian Bear and its Cossacks and the great British explorer.

Three firsts at almost a single stroke! Not bad going for the Gurkhas and these were early days yet.

Being central to these events, Younghusband, who had shot up from a captain to a colonel in double-quick time, had also made his first mark in the history of imperialism. The great explorer-soldier was no ordinary British officer. He published some twenty-eight books, including *The Heart of a Continent*, *Within*, *Wonders of the Himalaya*, *The Epic of Mount Everest*, *Life in the Stars*, *The Light of Experience*, *The Reign of God*, *The Living Universe*, *Modern Mystics* and *Wedding*. He preached free love, amongst other things, and was as interested in philosophy as he was military matters. He was not only a man of action, but a thinker and writer as well.

In 1919, Younghusband became president of the Royal Geographical Society and he was also founder-chairman of the Mount Everest Committee of mountain climbers. There can be no doubt that he was an enlightened thinker who was well ahead of his time. He was among those who looked forward to a world peace movement to break history's vicious cycle of war and, before his life was through, he campaigned for this.

It is worth noting that, just as the Gurkhas have always been more flexible and broad-minded than other Hindus, some of their British superiors in the officer class and elsewhere were themselves much more flexible than other Christians, at a time when there was no shortage of inflexible Christian men of war who were as fanatical as many of today's Muslim's fanatics who hate the West.

When, in 1857, the sepoys mutinied in India on religious grounds, because they were ordered to put the unholy cartridge grease into their mouths, the Gurkhas had no difficulty with this. On one occasion before the Indian Mutiny, they were sent the wrong grease and simply returned it to their British officers with an amusing note making light of the matter, and during the Mutiny itself they volunteered to bite the cartridges.

Younghusband was chief among those Britons who had good reason to admire the Gurkhas, not just for their abilities on the field of battle, but also for their mountaineering talents. He also had a healthy respect for the Gurkhas' religious animist belief in nature. The Gurkhas have long been perceived as a symbol of the mysterious spirituality in the Indian sub-continent, and in the company of a great mystic like Younghusband, they were in good company.

The Gurkhas' famously vacant laugh in the face of danger – whether on the battlefield or when confronted by life-threatening natural hazards in the harsh mountainous landscapes in Central Asia and their own homelands – must also have impressed Younghusband. Not that this famous laugh of theirs seems such an inappropriate response when, faced with all the terrors of hell, a man must somehow discover how best to keep up his spirit, if he is to survive to fight another day. Why would one not laugh at the extreme and irrational craziness of man? And why would one not want to keep one's spirit?

Military observers have pointed to the Gurkha's apparently ageless face, which sometimes seems to represent this spirituality, as does his open and fulsome smile, which not infrequently seems to come from his very soul. Maybe this is reading too much into Gurkha faces, but military men remark on it, time and again.

Another notable Gurkha characteristic is his selfless 'obedience' – which is what helps to make him such a good soldier, of course – but this obedience of his is said to be to the task or challenge in hand, rather than to the employer or leader. This selfless belief in service for its own sake, and the philosophy of 'as ye sow, so shall ye reap', are not such a mystery to the 'old style' Christian world with which Johnny Gurkha has long chosen to identify himself.

Interestingly, because the Gurkhas are committed to proving themselves by undertaking challenging or even impossible tasks, they are altogether a different animal than many other soldiers who, without strict discipline and orders, would not bother to complete the tasks that are set for them. Whilst the Gurkhas are subject to strict discipline, they also have great self-discipline, but more importantly the belief in doing a good job properly for its own sake and without being ordered to do so, or indeed seeking to be rewarded for it.

Of course, in their empire-building days in India and across its borders, the British had superior firepower, which it would have been remiss of them not to use. But they could handle themselves in hand-to-hand fighting with swords, daggers and bayonets as well, and that is why they were generally admired by the martial races of the sub-continent, and not least the Gurkhas, or their foes in Central Asia where they fought fearlessly and with great tenacity. It is worth remembering that when they conquered Tibet they were hopelessly outnumbered.

Taking time off from policing India, the Gurkhas went into

Central Asia with the first British explorer and soldiers who dared to show their white faces and pink noses in that part of the world.

# five

# HEARTBREAK IN INDIA

The British Army's admiration for its Gurkha soldiers, which had been growing for many decades, increased massively during the Indian Mutiny of 1857-8 when a mere 5,000 British troops found themselves at the mercy of 35,000 sepoys who hacked a great many British troops to death.

The mind boggles at the arrogant insensitivity of the British in insisting that, to load their rifles, Indian sepoys must bite off the end of cartridges greased with the fat of cows and pigs. Did they actually want a mutiny?

Prior to this crass insistence, there had been no shortage of British citizens in India who were not only tolerant of racial and religious differences, but positively in favour of many aspects Indian culture and its religions, from which they were keen to learn. They had preached a coming together of the different races and cultures that they found there. And in his novel *Kim*, Rudyard Kipling presented the most 'affectionate portraits' of India, to quote Geoffrey Moorhouse from his book *India Britannica*. So what went wrong?

Since Muslims regard pigs as unclean and Hindus regard cows as sacred, it is hard not to conclude that the British – until then so unjudgemental and careful – had temporarily taken leave of their senses. In Meerut, after they had chained eighty-five disobedient sepoys for refusing, on religious grounds, to bite the new cartridges – and after these deeply insulted men had been released by fellow sepoys – a frenzied rampage followed in which many British officers were killed.

The unrest spread to Cawnpore, Lucknow, Delhi and other cities throughout India. So the Gurkhas were swiftly called into action again, as a matter of extreme urgency. They found themselves marching up to thirty extremely hot miles a day in the scorching sun in order to reach and relieve or reinforce their besieged British masters, and along the way they were of course attacked by mutineers who ambushed and shot them. When the Gurkhas finally reached their destinations and joined up with the British, they were suffering from heat exhaustion, and when the mutineers called on them as fellow Asians to join the mutiny against the British, they pretended to be in favour, but only so that they could gain access to rebel strongholds, where they shot the mutineers dead.

The British felt immense affection for and gratitude to the Gurkhas, given the truly desperate situation in which they found themselves during the mutiny, which dragged on into a second year. During the siege of Delhi the Gurkha soldiers of the Sirmoor Rifles won no fewer than twenty-five Indian

Order of Merits for their bravery (twelve of which went to line boys), and the unit withstood a staggering twenty-six attacks. Having impressed the British in West Nepal and in the Sikh Wars of 1845–6 and 1848–9, the Gurkhas continued to do so during the Mutiny.

But today, when British television viewers and street crowds see Gurkha soldiers, in their familiar broad-rimmed scouts' hats, marching at British ceremonial occasions, most of them have no idea of the background to their country's relationship with the Gurkhas, or of the historical strength of the emotional bond.

The Gurkhas paid a heavy price for their support of the British during the Indian Mutiny, but they not only kept their chins up, they reportedly had some fun in the process, according to Tony Gould who tells us in *Imperial Warriors* that a 19-year-old British rifleman wrote home to his father saying: 'Yesterday, a sepoy had gone into a hut and was shooting out at the door, when two little Ghoorkas set out to catch him. They sneaked up, one on either side of the door, and presently the sepoy put out his head to see if the coast was clear, when one grabbed him by the hair, and the other whacked off his head with his cookery.'

Gould comments that 'war might be a grim business, a matter of kill or be killed (or maimed), but that was no reason to go about it grimly. Gurkhas approached it in a light-hearted manner and would extract what fun they could, no matter how serious the situation. They looked upon it as a kind of sport, or *shikar* (hunt).

By mid-July nearly half the Sirmoor battalion, 206 men, had

been killed or wounded, and on 19 July 'the twenty-first attack [...] by the "Pandies" [after Mangal Pande, the rebellious sepoy doped up on *bhang* whose violent behaviour and subsequent execution at Barrackpore had lit the fuse of mutiny] kept coming [...] as many as 10,000 or even 20,000 mutineers attacked [...] 910 [British Army] men in successive waves before they were finally forced to retreat.'

These days, ten or twenty thousand men against nine hundred is almost impossible to imagine. So too is wave after ceaseless wave of 21 attacks and more. And, with the Gurkhas losing half their men, one can perhaps see their need for keeping themselves together by turning Tony Gould's 'grim business' of warfare into a game or sport. Keeping war and death a light-hearted and even amusing matter seems central to the ethnic Gurkha soldier's ethos and amazing cool, but in the nightmare days of the Indian Mutiny this took a lot of doing.

When the Indian Mutiny was over, the British very sensibly abolished the East India Company, which had arguably brought it about, replacing the company, in its role as administrator of India and the East India Company Army, with British government administration. Before the incident that kick-started the Mutiny, there was always discontent and the possibility of such a revolt, but there is no doubt that the Company hastened events.

As anyone who has read the late J.G. Farell's novel *The Siege of Krishnapur* knows, things were desperate, terrifying and vile for the British during the Mutiny, not least because they found themselves overwhelmed and cut off by brutal and savage, marauding and heartless mutineers, who were on the rampage. This Booker Prize-winning work of fiction captures the atmosphere of combined horror, hopelessness and gallantry among the demoralised British at the merciless hands of the sepoys, who were 'lopping off the heads of Eurasians and planters as if they had been dandelions'. It also tells of the atrocious and sickening smells of putrefaction from dead men, women, horses and bullocks (not to mention the smells of unwashed bodies, urine and death among ailing British families under siege). Then there are the bloated birds, jackals and pariah dogs that gorge themselves on dead humans and animals alike. The novel describes how, during daytime, a vast crowd of Indian onlookers assemble on the slopes of a hill to enjoy the spectacle of a British residency being destroyed, as the Indians picnic and generally enjoy a day out with the accompaniment of sweet music and delicious-smelling Indian foods, while the British and Eurasians are being slaughtered. There is even talk among the British of 'shooting wives' if the situation becomes hopeless, 'to spare them a worse fate at the hands of the sepoys'. To understand exactly what the beleaguered British communities across India were up against, Farrell's book is essential (and compulsive) reading.

But, throughout the mutiny, Britain's faithful Gurkha friends never put a foot wrong, never did anything other than relieve the frightful agony of the British in every way that they could, repelling the horrors with, by all accounts, a dignity and occasional cavalier strength of purpose that left their British admirers even more astonished, wide-eyed, grateful and appreciative of their loyalty and bravery than before. When they were most needed, the trusty little Gurkhas were there again and again.

The following century, during the partition of India, the Gurkhas were still in the thick of it when needed, protecting Hindus and Muslims from one another. But why did they remain loyal to the British? Why didn't they switch sides once more, and become heroes all over again, this time in a different cause?

Well, the Gurkhas were paid, fed and clothed by the British, and provided with a decent roof over their heads. But escape from the dire poverty of Nepal cannot have been the only reason why these independently minded and hugely dignified soldiers chose to serve the British, who were not offering any land to this agricultural people.

It's important to remember that before their defeat by the East India Company Army – when they switched to the British side in 1817 – successive generations of Gurkhas had been a powerful force in their own right. Had they not liked what they found in British India, had they not warmed to their British overlords, these defiant and adventurous people could easily have broken ranks and escaped back to Nepal, taking their chances there, settling for a hard but less risky life, instead of sticking their necks out in the hot and dusty Punjab, against such ferocious warriors as the Sikhs, who had already rebuffed them once; and then again during the Indian Mutiny, when it looked to some, at least for a while, as if the days of the British in India might be numbered. Brian Lapping is in no doubt, in his book *End of Empire*, that with an estimated

257,000 Asian soldiers alongside 34,000 British, 'the Indians could have overwhelmed the British if they had wanted to. And in some places they did'.

But not all, or even most of them, wanted to, and the Gurkhas certainly did not want to. On the contrary, they were at one with their military comrades. For if the British had reason to be horror-struck at the prospect of being overwhelmed and massacred in the event of the Indian forces closing ranks and turning against them *en masse*, so too did their Gurkha accomplices. Nevertheless, in the face of this danger, the brave and dependable Gurkhas threw 8,000 men into the relief of Lucknow, up to their elbows in blood and gore alongside the British Army.

So there was no gun to Johnny Gurkha's head, nothing to keep him in British India, other than his liking for the British and what they were doing, and his liking for his active role in the British Army, which had clearly won his approval and respect as a fighting force and had looked after him sufficiently well into the bargain. Perhaps, very early on, he recognised that the well-organised and adventurous East India Company Army was going places, unlike the tribal and more parochial Gurkha Army back in Nepal.

It is also conceivable that Indians may have been less to Johnny Gurkha's taste than his white masters, in which case he would have had no difficulty siding with the British rather than his Asian neighbours and religious comrades beyond the Nepalese border, with whose cause he would not have identified. We know that he thought himself superior to the Indians, but we shall never know the full truth because early nineteenth-century historical records do not concern themselves with such matters. But what is manifestly clear is that he felt comfortable, indeed very much at home, with British fighting men. For he not only enjoyed their company, but also felt himself to be playing an important role in their military successes.

Fighting for and with the British fulfilled the Gurkhas by giving them a sense of self-belief and self-respect that perfectly suited this historic martial race. They felt that they were in good company – natural running mates of the leaders of the pack. At the outset of the relationship between Gurkha and British soldiers, both partners would instantly have understood the point made by Herbert Matthews in his book *The Education of a Correspondent*: 'war has ever been one of the primary functions of mankind and unless you see men fight you miss something fundamental.'

Sir Winston Churchill, in *The World Crisis*, said something similar – 'the story of the human race is war'; while Professor Arthur Marwick, in *War and Social Change in the 20th Century*, has written that 'it does not seem that either the psychologists or anthropologists have as yet agreed on a satisfactory theory of the causation of war, but undoubtedly one must look in the first instance at the nature of man himself'.

Despite their obvious racial and cultural differences, there was much in the warring nature of Gurkhas and Britons that made them surprisingly compatible.

A chapter in Marwick's book devoted to 'The Nature of the Problem' says: 'Much emphasis recently has been given to man's basic aggressive instincts. In the usage of Konrad

Lorenz, "aggression" … is a necessary part of human make-up, leading to the conquest of physical and other obstacles, without which the human race would not have achieved such progress as it has achieved. The problem is that the misapplication of aggressive instincts… manifestly has deep roots in human personality, whether natural or acquired; the political, economic and diplomatic "causes," which historians have been wont to argue over, stop short of telling the whole story. This means that in what must be the really crucial issue in any discussion of war and society – how do we prevent future wars? – the resources of psychology, social psychology, anthropology and sociology are probably more vital than those of history.'

In the nineteenth and twentieth centuries, when Gurkha and British soldiers were thronging to join the British Army to fight its battles around the world, they had no need of psychology or anthropology to guide their decision. Their instinctive intelligence – their native cunning – told them exactly what Churchill and Marwick have articulated: that they had bags of instinctive aggression for which a necessary outlet must be found, preferably in a good cause. In the view of both British and Gurkha soldiers of the British Army, 'human progress' was doubtless being advanced (at the same time as Britain, understandably, took the opportunity to line its pockets), whilst, between wars, man's petty aggression was being kept off the streets during the essentially peaceful development of civilisation. Whether to save democracy or to achieve justice or some ideological political goal, war was, in those days, generally regarded as 'normal' by most countries, including India, where the aggressive instinct not only prevails to this day, but is institutionalised in a giant military machine.

British and Gurkha soldiers alike would have readily understood the need for war in this wicked world, and they would have understood the fundamental 'whirl of experience' in relation to the Vietnam War referred to by Phillip Knightley in *The First Casualty* because virtually every warring tribe in the Indian sub-continent during those centuries was eager to give a bloody good battle a whirl and take a bloody good thrashing if necessary.

We are reminded by Knightley that, whether we like it or not, most brave men have been getting off on war for generations, just as the not-so-brave and the cowardly have been getting off on reading and writing about it, while thespians have got off on acting it out in plays and films. A phoney culture of war off the battlefield has reflected the appalling hunger of people for the dire and diabolical things that have been happening in the high drama of military conflict on the battlefield. While those on the touchline and in the audience, with their ugly fascination with violence and death, have argued endlessly about whether war is right or wrong, others in battledress have got on with it and fought the good fight, believing that it is either their job or their duty to do so, that they have no option *not* to do so. And given that their adrenalin has not let them down, Knightley points out that a high proportion of them have discovered that the 'exhilaration' of war has generally helped them to 'compensate' for the horror and counter much of the fear.

Many fighting men have discovered that war 'is fun', to

quote Nora Ephron's article 'The War Followers,' published in *New York* magazine in 1973. Using Ephron's 'war is fun' allegation for its title, Knightley has devoted a whole chapter of his book to this aspect of war. This truth is exactly what Johnny Gurkha was quick to discover in India in the service of the British, who enabled him to function at his battling best, in the days when the only substitute for the fantastic weaponry of today was fantastic guts and a cool head in the face of deadly aggression. The British provided the expertise and highly disciplined fun in which the Gurkhas excelled as gladiators extraordinaire. As the Gurkha officer Nigel Woodyat openly acknowledged in his book *Under Ten Viceroys*: 'There is nothing more fascinating than trans-border warfare. The wild and difficult country, the manly and hardy tribesman, the uncertainty regarding his movements, the element of surprise, the necessity for ceaseless vigilance, the calls that are made on the stamina of the troops and on one's own endurance, all tend to bewitch and allure… a very *dangerous sport*.'

It is hard to resist the conclusion that the Gurkhas and a goodly number of their British officers regarded soulless and dehumanising war as inevitable in this kill-or-be-killed world, so they adopted an attitude of 'why not make the most of it as a sporting activity in self-defence or conquest'. Why not have some manly enjoyment from it, as far as possible, for the thrill of the hunt, rather than fretting and worrying about it for the nasty and horrifying business that it actually is?

Other martial races in the Indian sub-continent and elsewhere had a similar philosophical attitude, but the Gurkhas went about it with a shrug and a sense of fun, with a determined smile on their faces, making the most of a grim business that was mad, bad and sad, and without complaining about or agonising over the consequences. This was, it seems, their way of accepting and dealing with the inevitable, and not letting it get them down or frighten them into submission. If, in reality, war was mad, bad and sad, the Gurkhas' reality was evidently, 'So what? It's got to be done, so give the enemy what he gives you, and never give in.' A wily sense of humour in such ugly and demeaning circumstances was no doubt their way of coping with the horror, just as it was in those days for so many British fighting men, who were equally determined not to be fussed, and who developed war as an 'art' as well as a sport (if war is all you know, your attitude to it is bound to be tailored accordingly). And this was not, where the British were concerned, simply a class or public school thing. The Gurkhas had not been to public school, any more than ordinary British soldiers or most warring Americans, Germans, Frenchmen and Japanese had been to such schools. But they all had an officer class and body of men who enjoyed a good fight.

Since the time of Ancient Rome, gladiators have fought beasts or other warriors in public, allowing cowardly onlookers to wonder at their bravery and admire their courage. And when the Gurkhas are thrown into the arena of war, like the gladiators they are, all eyes are upon them for the obvious reason that their reputation has gone before them and so much is expected from them, not infrequently against overwhelming or impossible odds. Like other crack troops – such as the SAS, the Paras and Commandos – the Gurkhas are expected to show what they can do, not just to the general public – in news reports, television coverage and books on war – but to other British soldiers who fight with them on the field of battle, so many of whom have said, for generations now, 'there's no other soldier I'd rather have alongside me than a Gurkha.'

Throughout the Gurkhas' embattled history, other soldiers – including their enemies, who have heard in advance of their prowess – have watched, applauded and written about them in glowing terms, and when the Gurkhas first came to Europe in the twentieth century they had a ready-made military audience that was waiting with keen interest to see if they could cope with a modern machine-age war. That audience was not disappointed, for the Gurkhas won ten of the twenty-six VCs awarded to Indian Army soldiers during the Second World War, even though they accounted for not more than one-fifth of the Indian Army presence. In the Olympic Games of War, the Gurkhas generally win a disproportionate number of gold medals.

And in the time-honoured tradition of gladiators, all crack troops, heroic airmen and sailors are still assured of an eager audience today. War films still attract the masses, and there has been heavy television coverage of wars such as Vietnam, the Falklands and the Gulf. And how many times has television shown us the SAS storming the Iranian Embassy in London? Books, dramas and television documentaries about the SAS, who operate in secret but cannot escape public attention, are by no means in short supply, because gladiatorial troops of this kind attract a cult following numbering hundreds of thousands.

As for the Gurkhas' fellow soldiers, few have ever been in serious doubt of their fighting qualities and virtues, and even Viscount Montgomery's reservations about soldiers from the Indian Army being able to cope in Europe are best explained, according to former Gurkha officer Tony Gould in the aforementioned *Imperial Warriors*, by 'Monty's failure to pass out of Sandhurst high enough to get into the Indian Army', which 'prejudiced him against it for life'.

Not that any of this adulation for the Gurkhas seems to have gone to their heads. They do not come over as macho, or obvious glory seekers On the contrary, they are modest and quietly confident, though they are, of course, unostentatiously very proud of themselves. No one could accuse them of being 'glory boys', which is doubtless part of the charm that these gentle gladiators have for their admirers.

When the University of London Sanskrit scholar and former soldier Sir Ralph MC Turner wrote in the preface of his 1930s Nepali Dictionary, of the 'stubborn and indomitable peasants of Nepal' disappearing 'into the smoke and wrath of battle' – when he referred to Johnny Gurkha as the 'bravest of the brave, most generous of the generous, never had a country more faithful friends than you' – he knew exactly what he was talking about, and most Gurkhas would have reciprocated this high regard for their British comrades in arms, who conducted themselves with a courage similar to their own, and with a poise, posture and bearing in uniform that made sense to them. The two, it seemed, were well met and well matched.

Of course, there comes a time when the fun is wiped from the face of war and turns into its opposite, a deadly and totally destructive nightmare too terrible to contemplate – as the Gurkhas, like other crack regiments renowned for their heroism, know to their cost. Yet, for all that, war never fails to erupt intermittently and attract its eager participants, which is why military minds firmly believe that they must always be in a state of preparation and readiness for it.

Man's eternal quest for political and colonial dominance is as old as history, although in exploring Johnny Gurkha's story we have only to go back to the early nineteenth century and to a particularly murderous and extremely harsh part of the world where the Great Game added another dimension to long-standing tribal conflicts. When, for example, the British entered into the Sikh Wars, it was because local unrest between Sikh warlords, who were battling against one another, might have given the Russians the pretext and opportunity they needed to intervene and acquire a presence in India. As it was, the British settled the Sikhs' hash, forestalling Russian ambitions.

The Gurkhas of Nepal, with their native cunning, had a shrewd understanding of these tricky matters, and they may well have concluded that, while such odious things as racist colonisation, slavery and the class system were not invented by the British, there was no one to touch them in such endeavours once they got their act together and imitated the ways of others. They may have come to the view that the British were better at imperialism and at military ritual than other nations, and that they had embarked on a grand adventure that they, the Gurkhas, did not want to miss. Also, they may have decided that, having fought for and against the

British, they preferred the devil they knew to other potential colonisers of the sub-continent, such as the Russians, French, Dutch, Portuguese and Japanese (interestingly the Japanese, like the Chinese after them, got nowhere fast against Indian warriors by whom they were defeated and turned back). For that matter, the Gurkhas may well have preferred the British to the Indians, who obviously had a head start on the British with their exploitative caste system, as did the Muslim invaders, who had been seasoned slave traders and had converted Indians to Islam by the sword. Once the British had shown their white faces in a part of the world where a white skin was a novelty – and, more to the point, demonstrated what a ferocious mob they too could be on the world's most ghastly battlefields – it is not impossible that it was the 'style' of their colonialism, warfare and class system that mattered most to the Gurkhas and others, and not so much the content, which did not bother them greatly. Today such a view would be regarded as being as preposterous as it is politically incorrect, but it would not have been either of these things back in the early nineteenth century.

In the fierce competition between the proud Indian regiments that served the British Raj, Johnny Gurkha was regarded by the British as incomparable, with the Sikhs not far behind (not that the warrior Sikhs have ever regarded themselves a close second to anyone, least of all the Gurkhas!) Having fought with the British in two bloodthirsty wars against the Sikhs, the Gurkhas had proved themselves in British India, rising to the fearsome challenge with the same skill and bravery that they had shown in their first fight against the British themselves some thirty years earlier. But the Gurkhas had proved themselves to be not only ferocious fighters, but also amenable to discipline, strong in patience and fortitude, and utterly dependable. Also, nobody had heard of any accusations of theft or dishonesty levelled at the Gurkhas, most of whom would have been deeply insulted by such a charge. They were, it seemed, honourable men, who regarded bloody warfare as perhaps the most honourable activity of all. It was Johnny Gurkha's dependability and loyalty to the British cause that was to go such a long way in enabling the British to police the teeming millions of the sub-continent – not least during two World Wars, when the Gurkhas poured 16,000 troops into India while its absent landlord was away fighting the Germans.

Although the Gurkhas and the British, fighting alongside one another, came out on the winning side in the two Sikh Wars – which were a close-run thing because the Sikhs were, like the Gurkhas, formidable warriors – the victorious British made friends with the defeated Sikhs too, enlisting them as worthy soldiers to fight alongside them (to this day the Sikhs remain a feared and an elite fighting force in the Indian Army, second only, perhaps, to the Anglo-Indian forces.) And like the Gurkhas before them, the Sikhs acknowledged the British as first-class men of war and worthy colonisers. They too did not find it difficult to serve the British, whom they respected as a martial race.

Of course the mixed-blood Anglo-Indians were the most loyal to the British cause, having British blood in their veins and, in most cases, hearts in their bodies. But, to begin with, they were far too clever and successful for their British masters, demonstrating a brainpower and a military ability that did not inevitably need British leadership. Robert Clive had been succeeded by an Anglo-Indian commander-in-chief, Sir Eyre Coote, while India's most famous and best cavalry regiment, Skinner's Horse, had been founded by the aforementioned heroic Anglo-Indian officer with an Indian Rajput mother. Every white English officer arriving in India wanted to be in James Skinner's 'Yellowboys', who considered themselves entirely superior to mere infantrymen footslogging their way into battle, and made no exception for the Gurkhas or any other infantry regiments.

General Sir John Hearsey, who acted wisely on the eve of the Mutiny by advising the authorities to let the sepoys provide their own grease for their cartridges, had an Indian Jat mother.

Clearly the mixed race that the British East India Company had encouraged as a matter of policy was in danger of leaving the British behind in certain fields, and this had caused many of the latter to become jealous and uneasy. The benefactor of Yale University in the United States, Elihu Yale, the former governor of Madras, had been married to a woman of mixed blood.

These Anglo-Indians were doing too well for themselves and, to Britain's everlasting shame, there was jealousy on the British side, as a result of which, steps were taken between 1786 and 1795 to bar Anglo-Indians from the coveted ranks of the civil service and from all military rank, except in the capacity of bandsmen and farriers!

This was as incredible as it was shameful and, to this day, many Anglo-Indians find it hard to forgive the British.

No new mixed blood was to be allowed in the services of the East India Company, and this shabby treatment was to be underlined within a few years when, being in desperate need of all the manpower it could muster to fight the Marathas and Hyder Ali in Mysore, the Company appealed to Anglo-Indians yet again, to fight alongside full-blooded Britons and Indian sepoys, and was not disappointed by the patriotic response. But it then proceeded to disband them as soon as the last shot was fired! This disgraceful process was regularly repeated, right through to the Indian Mutiny, whenever battle had to be fought. Yet the British still managed to get the kind-hearted loyalty of these worthy Anglo-Indians, the latter of whom got precisely nowhere in the upper ranks of the British army, by return, and this is a stain that remains on British military history to this day.

Not until 1858, in the aftermath of the mutiny, did the vast majority of Anglo-Indians cease to be social outcasts, for it was then that the British finally came off their high horse and did their condescending best to make amends by rewarding their blood brothers and sisters for their loyalty. They did this grudgingly, by introducing a new racially determined employment policy that enabled Anglo-Indians to rise to the rank of sergeant in the British Army – but not any higher! – and to run the railways, work in customs and excise, posts and telegraphs, and eventually to become sufficiently well educated to become doctors (as it happens, I have an Oxford University educated third-generation Anglo-Indian niece who is a doctor). They also became technologists, systems analysts, accountants, engineers and school teachers Today in India there are Anglo-Indian pilots and naval and army commanders. Although the Anglo-Indians had served the British every bit as loyally as Johnny Gurkha – and matched and sometimes surpassed him on the field of battle – they had not yet received proper recognition as junior partners of the British in their great Indian adventure. And, to make matters worse for the Anglo-Indians, the Muslims – with their strict religious beliefs, moral judgements and codes – regarded them as impure and were in no mood to forgive them for their mixed blood, while many Hindus also treated them as social outcasts. What the Anglo-Indians had done to deserve such treatment remains a mystery to this day, except to say that we all know how sensitive most races are about mixed blood, however capable and brilliant the offspring.

Yet it was Ochterlony's Anglo-Indian foresight that first got the Gurkhas into favour, a mission in which he was ably supported by Lieutenant Frederick Young, who was reportedly captured by Gurkha soldiers and spoke so highly of them.

But as far as Johnny Gurkha was concerned, he was, in the eyes of his British masters, the supreme infantryman, elevated above all the others and at least equal to the Anglo-Indians and their famous Skinner's Horse. He was pleased as punch with his prestige and proud to serve the British Crown. And he was secure in the knowledge that any British Army officer going to India with kudos in mind would, given his pick, opt for a crack Gurkha regiment, as so many of the most famous and distinguished British officers did (and as Britain's Viscount Montgomery, for example, was not sufficiently qualified at Sandhurst to do). No doubt about it, Gurkha regiments in India were the crème de la crème and most top British officers wanted to join them: unless, of course, they were in the cavalry, in which case they would probably choose the 'Yellowboys'. There were also the famous Guides, who were an unusual combination of infantry and cavalry.

It was a shrewd but nevertheless genuine move by the British to pay tribute to Johnny Gurkha in this way. And it was even shrewder of them to have built and managed what now looks like the biggest and perhaps the first modern multinational army of coloured races and cultures in relatively modern times – so magnificent in its ceremonial splendour and pageantry, yet ruthlessly effective when called upon to fight. Whilst other invading armies had co-opted soldiers from other races as they made their way around the world – and the French Foreign Legion had accepted recruits from different countries into an essentially French legion – the British had founded, managed, pay-rolled and trained a vast multinational and multicultural fighting machine, in which served Indians, mixed-race Anglo Indians, Pakistanis, Bengalis, Sikhs, Afghans, Nepalese, Irish, Scottish, English and European (before some of these countries had been founded).

This was a charismatic fighting force that made a lot of people proud, not least the Gurkhas.

And what a spectacular and spellbinding army it was! What an extraordinary and exciting home-grown fighting unit acting in support of a much smaller army of occupation. How could any red-blooded soldier, least of all Johnny Gurkha, not be seduced and enchanted by it all, and almost bursting with quietly controlled pride to be a part of it?

He couldn't, of course, and this goes a long way in explaining the loyalty of the Gurkhas to the British in India. They could not break the spell and flee from the power of the enchanter. The Gurkhas loved it, and they loved Britain's Indian Army, which disciplined and trained them, masterminding their role in the great events of the Raj.

The Pathans were up there with the Gurkhas, Sikhs, Rajputs and Anglo-Indians as fearsome and deadly fighters, and it was into this bloodthirsty arena that the British pitched Johnny Gurkha, giving him the time of his life. There was no place for lack of nerve, resolve or character in these violent and dangerous times. One had to be a fearless and brutal warrior through and through, with nerves of steel and a taste for heroism. The challenges set by the British really tested and stretched the Gurkhas, taking them all the way to hell and back. It was an arrangement that perfectly suited this martial people's courageous and warring temperament, and it explains much of the devotion and loyalty of the Gurkhas to the British in India.

But if the Gurkhas were impressed by the ability of the British to conceive this awesome army of many races, they must surely have been no less impressed by their ability to get on with the various groups of native warriors and keep them all happy. No wonder the Gurkhas, like the Sikhs and other warriors in India, were full of admiration for the British, not only for their prowess as fighting men, but also for the transparent British justice they brought to a part of the world where what precious little there was of this commodity was a very murky affair. They could see with their own eyes that 'judicious fathering' and 'mature consideration' for defeated armies and tribes were winning friends and influencing native peoples, just as they had in their own lands in west Nepal.

While the British were extending their empire into India in order to rob the sub-continent of its great wealth before other Western powers did so, they were also taking care not to rub salt into the wound (which is why it is hard to explain the behaviour that triggered the Mutiny, or indeed the British attitude to its mixed race Anglo-Indians). On the contrary, they were showing Indians, Sikhs and Gurkhas their due share in the reflected glory of empire and there can be no doubt that this appealed to them. Even the most ardent critics of the British Raj have a hard time disproving this. Of course, as we now know, it was all destined to end in tears, but this was not for want of the British trying to get things right in India. Flawed the British may have been, but they did have a good try at putting things right, putting their own wrongs to right. To put the unashamed bribery and corruption and unjust rule of the heady days of Robert Clive and the East India Company behind it, Britain was bending over backwards to be just, even-handed and squeaky clean in its dealings with the natives. It was also offering them access to a culture that had the advantage of 'knowledge… stored in books… like hermetically sealed provisions waiting for the day when you may need a meal... a culture so flexible that whatever [was] needed was there in a book...' as we are reminded by Farrell in *The Siege of Krishnapur*. And the fancy did take the intelligent and culture-loving Indians and mixed-race Anglo-Indians, most of whose intelligentsia are, to this day, too intelligent, cultured and honest not to acknowledge the contribution of British culture to their own development.

So it was all this, quite apart from the economic considerations and the reassurance that there was no British military threat to the Gurkha kinfolk back in their homeland of Nepal, that had captured the hearts and appealed to the imaginations of Britain's Gurkha soldiers, just as it was doing among native Indian forces, as the British ran more and more of the sub-continent with their approval and help. It was this clever psychology and even-handedness that worked the magic for the British during most of their time in India before the Mutiny. And when the magic failed occasionally, 'dear old Johnny Gurkha' could be relied upon not to desert his British masters.

Admiration gives pleasure and satisfaction to the person who feels it for another, for whatever reason, and it can cause a seductive sense of wonder even when the other person is a rival or enemy. Mutual admiration can transcend racial and other differences between opposites, even on the field of battle, and lead to the creation of a strong bond between them, and this is what happened between the British and both the Gurkhas and the Sikhs. Field Marshal Viscount Sir William Slim was a great admirer of the Gurkhas, before he served with them, and his 1950s book *Defeat into Victory* is an interesting read for military historians and soldiers. He reports that he 'first met the 6th Gurkha Rifles in 1915 in Gallipoli. There I was so struck by their bearing in one of the most desperate battles in history that I resolved, should the opportunity come, to try to serve with them. Four years later it came, and I spent many of the happiest, and from a military point of view, the most valuable years of my life in the Regiment.'

Gallipoli came a century after British and Gurkha soldiers had first begun to form impressions of one another in Nepal and India. But, one might ask, if such mutual admiration existed between these fighting men in those days, how come worthy Gurkhas – or Anglo-Indian men at arms, for that matter – couldn't become officers and gentlemen like their British counterparts? The answer is, I believe, sadly and infuriatingly political, and in no way detracts from this theory of admiration.

The mutual admiration between the Gurkhas and the British suffered a serious blow when independence came in 1947 and the politicians upset the applecart. Suddenly there were clear signs that the love affair was in deep trouble, that the enchantment was showing every sign of breaking.

At this time there were some ten Gurkha regiments in business in British India, but only four of them was allowed to stay under the British flag, while the remaining six were transferred to the new Indian flag and told that they must remain in India. This meant that four would have to leave the country, never to return (they went to Malaya), while the rest would stay in India under Indian Army officers.

Gurkha soldiers were asked to choose whether to stay with their British or Indian regiments, and since they could not all transfer to only four British regiments, the majority did not have much choice. If they wanted to carry on soldiering they would have to choose the Indian Army regiments under Indian officers whether they liked it or not.

The Gurkhas were heartbroken and furious about this, as were many of their British officers, who could do nothing about the meddling of crass politicians, except cry 'shame' and 'a bloody disgrace' in the officers' mess. It seemed to the Gurkhas that, after all their loyalty to the British, they were being handed over, left behind, and that if they knew what was good for them they had better make the most of it in India. Predictably this embittered quite a lot of Gurkhas, who could not believe that the much-admired British, their beloved senior partners, would agree to leave so many of their Gurkha regiments behind. Some of them were so angry that, when their colonel turned up to wish them farewell, they spat in his face and shouted pro-Indian and anti-British slogans.

With British officers turning their backs on their Gurkha soldiers, walking out on them without so much as a by your leave – and with the no longer all-powerful British Raj now in disarray – the Gurkhas, who had recently helped the British defeat the Germans and Japanese, could not believe that they were being abandoned. Of course they were resentful and angry. Who wouldn't be? They felt treacherously betrayed.

What was happening was a crying shame. Men were being painfully separated from their beloved regiments, as a result of which the Gurkha Army was having its heart cut out, not by the *kukri*, but by the more exacting surgical scalpel of modern politics. It was time for the Gurkhas to grow up and throw up.

The British had traditionally denied commissions to their more able Gurkha soldiers on the grounds that discipline was better maintained by their own very capable white Gurkha officers, who had led by fearless example and whom the Gurkhas themselves openly acknowledged as the bravest and best leaders of men they had come across. And when the time came for those Gurkhas that could to choose between a British or Indian army, the British, to their everlasting shame, still denied them commissions. But there were others, and not least the new Indian government, who thought that the British were at heart racist in their refusal to grant Gurkhas officer status. The Indians shrewdly expected that the British would finish up sacrificing their cause for a foolish racist principle, and this is exactly what they did. The Gurkhas had, of course, felt insulted when asked to choose between Britain and India, because they believed that, after all they had done for them, their masters should not put them in such a needless position. But they were doubly insulted when they discovered that the British didn't rate them as highly as the Indians did, when it came to promoting them to the officer class. The Gurkhas were also irked by some Indians who looked down on them as soldiers of fortune who could be bought at the right price.

In the end, the majority of Gurkhas stayed in India, either out of disgust with their British masters or in order to get a commission, not to mention the impossible nature of the so-called choice that they were asked to make; while all of them, including those who chose British Gurkha regiments, suffered a big loss of innocence.

The love affair had cooled, but was it really over?

# six

# BITING THE BULLET IN THE TWENTIETH CENTURY

After India gained Independence in 1947, there was never any shortage of Gurkhas to continue biting the bullet for their British masters for the remainder of the twentieth century. So the famous love affair was destined to continue.

It had, it seemed, survived for the majority of Gurkha soldiers.

After they had spent the first half of the century cutting their teeth in British India – and fighting for Britain in the First and Second World Wars – it was thought that those Gurkhas who remained with British regiments (as well as the new recruits who continued to enlist) could be used to very good effect in other theatres of war outside India.

They could continue to growl and snarl for the British cause in what was to be the most warring century known to history: two World Wars, including the jungle warfare in

Burma, the Cold War, Vietnam and a host of other lesser but nevertheless damaging and demanding wars and policing exercises in various parts of the world.

So the Gurkhas were still in business, with or without British India, and Europe and the West was becoming familiar with their fighting qualities.

Heroic and enduring in action, full of the will to win and, more importantly, the stubborn will not to lose – triumphant in victory and defiant in retreat or defeat, refusing to lie down and die, dying and suffering with courage and dignity, and perhaps even cheerfully – all these are supposed to be the essential qualities required of the best fighting men, and the Gurkhas were soon demonstrating that they had such qualities in abundance. (As, of course, did their comrades in arms the British, forever a martial race, just like the Gurkhas, so why wouldn't this extraordinary and curious love affair continue?)

Both British and Gurkha warriors understood perfectly well that it's not just being macho, or winning heroically or romantically, that counts on the field of battle. It's enduring heroically too, without complaint, and never giving up, but always growing up fast where violence is concerned. It's no good simply lusting after glory, because in reality one has to suffer and work very hard to earn it, and there is always a painful price to be paid, which may or may not be worth it. One has to draw strength from heroism in defeat as well as in victory. There is a balance to be achieved between these essential qualities that make up the all-round fighting man, a balance of opposites, and this was no mystery to either

Gurkha or British soldiers. Yet apparently it was to the Argentinian soldiers who invaded the Falkland Islands in 1982, for their macho and sloppy concept of warrior heroism did not include these sterling qualities, although, to be fair to the inexperienced young teenage soldiers, they had their officers to blame for much of this. (On the other hand, inexperienced young Gurkha boys from the hills of west Nepal have for generations shown a greater maturity and will to win, with or without training.)

As the century moved on, Johnny Gurkha found himself far from Indian shores, in distant parts of the world where the weather was for much of the time not hot and dusty, but freezing cold, snowbound, wet, damp and cloudy. And he was exposed to gloomy and grimy industrialised places where the warfare was likewise heavily industrial and mechanised. It was no longer sunny, adventurous and wild – a dangerous sporting activity carried on up in the hills and mountain slopes or down in the sun-drenched flatlands – but a dark and nightmarish activity in muddy landscapes, blitzed by bombs, rockets, grenades, dynamite, high explosives, poisonous gases and extremely heavy artillery. Now trench warfare, tanks, big guns and machine guns, aeroplanes, anti-aircraft guns and shell shock were the components of a new kind of lethal game for the Gurkhas, in which paratroopers fell from the skies, armed to the teeth and ready to bayonet or shoot the enemy to death, and commandos, SAS and other special-forces soldiers undertook all manner of high-risk and impossible tasks on land and at sea.

This machine-age war, to which the Gurkhas were entirely

unaccustomed, was also deafening beyond belief, so noisy and ear-splitting that it made a man's nerves jangle like a skeleton's bones, often before he had the opportunity to fire a single shot. And no doubt to Johnny Gurkha's distaste, it was the kind of war that did all in its crushing power to thwart the individualism of the brave and heroic soldier. For he could be killed from a cowardly distance by a stray missile, bomb or bullet triggered by almost any idiot who may be neither brave nor heroic, nor even a good shot. Nor did he even see the whites of his enemies' eyes, for many of them no longer had the courtesy to make themselves known and prove that they were qualified to kill their opponents in hand-to-hand fighting.

In Gurkha eyes, it was all bound to be so impersonal and unfriendly, this mug's game of industrial war. Where was the satisfaction to be found? What use were gladiators here?

It is estimated that at least 100,000 Gurkhas fought in the First World War, from 1914 to 1918, of whom between 10,000 and 20,000 were killed or injured, while 2,000 won awards for gallantry. Gallons of Gurkha blood drenched European battlefields in this war that was supposed to end all wars, in France, Italy, Gallipoli and Mesopotamia.

In industrial warfare the Gurkhas had much to acclimatise themselves to, as they put their reputation as wild frontiersmen and mountain soldiers behind them (but not, of course, their *kukris*, which still had their uses after the heavy industry of war had run its course in the initial stages of a battle), and they realised that the 'scenic' war to which they were entirely accustomed was long gone.

All grades of human courage – with which Johnny Gurkha was so well endowed – were no longer appreciated by the majority of people in the mid to late twentieth century. On the contrary, courage seemed to be regarded as highly suspect – both morally and intellectually – and woefully wrong-headed. A ceaselessly embattled world had had more than enough of human courage from men of war, whose fighting qualities were out of favour, and whose valour had become a discredited and unpopular ideal with people who hoped that, fingers crossed, if nations did not think about war, it would kindly go away and leave them alone.

According to Andrew Rutherford, in *The Literature of War*: 'The assumption that heroism, like saintliness, is obsolete as an ideal, and that the literature of heroism belongs to the childhood of the individual or of the race, seems typical of current intellectual opinion. Fortitude is out of fashion as a virtue. Indeed the portrayal of courage in the face of adversity, suffering or danger is now positively suspect in the eyes of many readers, whose unexamined ethical assumptions often predetermine their aesthetic judgments (leading them, for example, to see Falstaff's views on Honour as more normative than Hal's, or to discount war poetry when it is not anti-war) … such cynicism … can also function … to expose false sentiment, hypocrisy or error, but it fails disablingly to take account of the basic dualism of human nature analysed by Orwell in "The Art of Donald McGill": "There is one part of you that wishes to be a hero or a saint, but another part of you is a little fat man who secs very clearly the advantages of staying alive with a whole skin. He is your unofficial self, the voice of the belly protesting against the soul.'"

Commenting on the anti-heroic bias of so many modern readers – and the paradox of the all-too-human refusal of people to be heroic – Rutherford argues that 'literature which explores this paradox deserves more critical attention than it currently receives.'

In the late twentieth century, an era of anti-heroism and boring machine-age war, the Gurkhas had reinvented themselves as men of war. And Doubting Thomases who were not yet convinced of their ability to adjust as well to industrial wars as they had always adjusted to the non-industrial variety were soon proved wrong.

Even before Indian Independence, some Gurkhas had first had a taste of industrial warfare with the British during the First World War, where it had taken a bit of time for them to get the hang of trench warfare. Together with the British on the Western Front, they had struggled and suffered, but at Flanders they finally 'did their duty and found their Valhalla', as we are told in the *Historical Record of the 6th Gurkha Rifles*. Eighty-six of 120 Gurkhas were killed or wounded at Loos in 1915 when rifleman Kulbir Thapa won a VC for fighting his way, with a small group of Gurkhas, into the German trenches and becoming the only one to return. And he did not return empty-handed. On his way back he rescued two Gurkha soldiers under fire, and he brought a wounded British soldier with him under the German wire, even though he was wounded himself.

Captain Grimshaw noted in *Imperial Warriors* that: 'The

state of the wounded beggars all description. Little Gurkhas slopping though the freezing mud barefooted, Tommies with no caps on and plastered with blood and mud from head to foot, Sikhs with their hair all down and looking more wild and weird than I have ever seen them, Pathans more dirty and untidy than usual, all limping and reeling along like drunken men... misery depicted in their faces... I stopped some Gurkhas and asked why they walked in bare feet. Those that replied said, "Sahib, our feet hurt terribly, but in boots they hurt worse."'

To add insult to injury, Gurkha clothing was disgracefully inadequate and they did not get greatcoats and serge uniforms until after they had arrived in France, at the end of winter, when spring was about to begin. And the European trenches in which they found themselves for the first time were too deep for these men who were, on average, no more than five-and-a-half feet tall.

According to Sir Ian Hamilton in the *Historical Record*, if he had been given more Gurkhas at the Dardanelles, he 'would never have been held up by the Turks'. It was at Gallipoli that Australian, New Zealand and British troops were massacred on a suicidal mission that was botched from the start. But it is a fascinating lesser-known fact that the Gurkhas were the only allied soldiers to succeed in defeating the Turks there. Commenting on the aforementioned Colonel Bruce, who led his Gurkhas at Gallipoli, Major Allanson is quoted in Tony's Gould's *Imperial Warriors* as saying: 'He is a fine optimistic man, with but few complaints; he has been about seven weeks in the Gallipoli Peninsula, and said from start to finish the whole thing was one long nightmare. Shell, maxim and rifle fire, to say nothing of bombs, without intermission, and that for periods of over a fortnight it had been impossible even to take off one's boots or stockings. He said we suffered from a shortage of machine guns and bombs, the latter being nearly all locally made in the Peninsula, and were fighting a very brave enemy, well equipped and in magnificently defended positions.'

Bruce is described by Gould as 'a legendary figure in his time, a famous mountaineer, a man of enormous physical strength and prodigious appetites', who was said by some to have 'screwed every Gurkha wife in the battalion'. But, Gould observes, 'if true, this was certainly unusual: British officers generally kept well away from Gurkha wives; apart from disciplinary considerations they had too much respect for their men to risk provoking their anger. But Bruce seems to have enjoyed breaking the rules. It was he who started the *khud* or hill race at which Gurkhas excel. Because of their size, they found it impossible to compete on equal terms with Sikhs and Punjabi Muslims in most forms of athletics; so in order to prevent them developing a sporting inferiority complex, Bruce introduced hill running. Though himself an excellent cross-country runner, he had noticed that the Gurkhas could easily outstrip him ... and rightly assumed they would outstrip everyone else.' Gould also explains that Bruce, nicknamed *Bhalu* the Bear because of his size and strength, was 'essentially a free spirit ... fluent in the [Gurkha] language and familiar with his men'.

In the climax of the campaign against the Turks, Allanson

led his Gurkhas into battle and recorded, we learn from *Imperial Warriors*, that: 'At the top we met the Turks: Le Marchand went down, a bayonet through the heart. I got one through the leg, and then, for about ten minutes, we fought hand to hand, we bit and fisted, and used rifles and pistols as clubs: blood was flying about like spray from a hairwash bottle. And then the Turks turned and fled, and I felt a very proud man; the key of the whole peninsula was ours, and our losses had not been so very great for such a result.'

But this famous victory, which ought to have been a turning point in favour of the Allies, was short-lived because in the absence of fresh troops the position that the Gurkhas and their British officers had taken from the Turks (who were commanded by German officers) could not be secured; and matters were not helped when, according to Allanson, the Royal Navy mistook the Gurkhas for Turks and shelled them. This – in addition to a fierce counter-attack by the Turks – resulted in the Gurkhas being dislodged from the ridge that they had fought so well to secure.

There were 60,000 heavily armed Turkish troops awaiting British, Australasian, French and Gurkha regiments at Gallipoli, with the supreme advantage of having machine gunners dug in high above the invading forces, in steep hills and at the top of rocks ranging in height from 330 to 7,000 feet. So it was not difficult for the Turks to effortlessly mow down the enemy as they ran for cover, which was almost impossible to find in the scrubby terrain beneath the commanding heights. Exposed without cover, the British were throwing men into the Turkish gunfire, without regard for their protection, and losing between 7,000 and 12,000 at a time in separate operations, while the Turks, who had the upper hand, were reckoned to be losing about 10,000 per week. The invasion was generally agreed to be suicidal and foolhardy, wrong-headed from the start thanks to the British War Cabinet (Messrs Winston Churchill and Lloyd George) and a good number of army and naval commanders who failed to get their act together. Invaders who survived the Turkish guns and shells had to climb, scramble or run up the sides of the steep and impregnable inclines, and engage in hand-to-hand fighting with the Turks, and the fact they were well used to this no doubt explains why the Gurkhas became the first and only allied soldiers to succeed in taking a Turkish highpoint after the Royal Marines and Dublin Fusiliers had been beaten off. In close-quarters fighting with the Turks, the Gurkhas decapitated twelve of them and shot many more, while losing eighteen of their own men and suffering forty-seven injuries.

Penned in on the beachheads, the allied forces were not making much headway until a night attack on the summits of the Sari Bair ridge – a mountain range running parallel to the sea – resulted in the capture of 150 Turks after cliff-climbing invaders took them by surprise.

Both sides lost hundreds of thousands of men, not only in the wrath of battle, but also to disease and ill-health. Men were freezing to death or drowning in their flooded trenches, when they were not being shot or hacked to death. The resilience of the Gurkhas was simply amazing.

In the end, the Allies decided that enough was enough, so they pulled out under cover of darkness, quietly evacuating the peninsula at night and retreating on Royal Navy ships, without the Turks realising that they were gone. It was one of the biggest fiascos and most inglorious failures of British military history, but, yet again, the Gurkhas came out with full honours.

By now Johnny Gurkha was held in the highest esteem, not just in British India, but in Europe as well. His credibility had rocketed, not least on account of the 8th Gurkhas' performance at Loos, in France, and the 6th Gurkha Rifles becoming the only troops in the whole Gallipoli campaign to reach and hold the crest line at Sari Bair and look down on the Straits from that commanding height (which, as it happens, was the ultimate objective of the disastrous and otherwise failed invasion).

It is against this distinguished and adventurous background that, in December 1993, a Gurkha statue was unveiled by the Queen of England in Horse Guards Avenue, off London's Whitehall. Sculpted by Philip Jackson, this work has since inspired statuette reproductions, about twelve inches high, in resin bronze, and mounted on a wooden base, for decorative and/or display purposes in homes, offices and military premises. Clearly, the twentieth century was the one in which the Gurkhas had finally arrived in Britain and Europe, with a permanent commemoration to their gallantry in the heart of London, close to the seat of government. They were no longer distant and shadowy warriors from mysterious foreign parts, but part of the furniture of the streets of London, publicly acknowledged and remembered along with all the other warriors in Britain's long military history, in whose honour such statues and memorials have been erected.

Even so, it had been a long, hard slog for the Gurkhas to achieve a place in the annals of British history. Western troops – German, Italian, French, Turkish, American, Canadian, as well as Australasian, were getting an eyeful of Johnny Gurkha for the first time, and they were discovering, as the British already knew, that this little guy was a soldier and a half. Just as twentieth-century soldiers from Europe, North America and Australasia had become acquainted with the Gurkhas for the first time on the field of battle, twentieth-century tourists and other visitors from those countries were becoming aware of them when visiting London and seeing the Gurkha statue.

For Hitler's Germans in particular, the Gurkhas had arrived in Europe to give them a wake-up call. The Germans could not believe their eyes or their ears as hundreds of their soldiers surrendered to this little brown man from a Far Eastern 'master race' as they watched their soldiers being killed and captured in action by these Asian soldiers.

In Mesopotamia (Iraq and eastern Syria) the Second World War was being fought to safeguard oil fields in Persia (Iran) and to forge a link with the Arabian Gulf and Suez. But, once again, there were too many ferocious Turks in the way, assisted by Arab conscripts. Against overwhelming odds, British and Gurkha troops poured into Mesopotamia, where Turkish heads soon began to roll as the Gurkhas hacked their way through their ranks. But not for long, because too many Turkish reinforcements arrived, and the British and Gurkha soldiers soon found themselves outnumbered, outgunned and cut off. The futile British campaign was terribly misguided and, in the absence of any reinforcements of their own to relieve them, brave but besieged British, Gurkha and Indian soldiers found themselves surrendering to the enemy – 2,600 Britons and 10,486 of the latter. Like Gallipoli before it, Mesopotamia turned out to be a fiasco – another botched campaign – until the Turks were eventually overrun when 166,000 Allied soldiers, including 110,000 Gurkhas, were sent to put matters right. This they did, though far too late. By now the Gurkhas had an unaccustomed audience of Turks, Germans and Arabs.

With the Second World War over, the Gurkhas were, throughout the rest of the twentieth century, always in the forefront of wars fought by Britain and India respectively. But it was in the war against the Japanese in Burma that the Gurkhas had had an awful lot of bullet to bite.

It was in Burma that, together with other British regiments, the Gurkhas were part of Britain's 'Forgotten Army' (as Mountbatten called it), but under Field Marshal Slim, who had resolved at Gallipoli that he would lead them one day, that army found a new sense of purpose.

The war in Burma was an epic drama and it is surprising that it has been overlooked by Hollywood's film-makers. *Bridge On the River Kwai* is only a small part of a story that remains lost to contemporary drama, even more than it has been lost to history.

And it's not only a British drama that we are talking

about here. It is also an Indian drama, because there was no shortage of Indian troops involved in the magnificent defeat of the Japanese. There were Sikhs, mixed-race Anglo-Indians, Madrassies, Pathans and so on, giving the Japanese the biggest bloody nose of their lives. This was the 250-year-old Honourable East India Company Army, transformed and updated for modern warfare, reminding the Japanese – who had been victors in China and Singapore – that in Burma they had bitten off more than they could chew. India may have had enough of British Imperialists, but it was certainly in no mood to tolerate Japanese imperialists. This was India's soldiers, and not just Johnny Gurkha, standing by the British at a time when they could easily have defected to the invading Japanese.

And, more to the point, it was Indian soldiers proving that they could deal with the Japanese, with or without the aid of the British. Unlike Vietnam a few decades later, this was an epic drama that ended in a convincing victory – not for imperialism, because the British were already making plans to move out of India.

Full credit has never been given to Britain and India for what they finally achieved in Burma against one of the fiercest and most ruthless foes known to mankind. On the contrary, emphasis has been put on the humiliation of the British in Singapore (and of the Chinese in China) at the murderous hands of the brave but sadistic Japanese. But there is much more to the story than this, and the much that is missing is the untold drama of what happened in Burma.

In order to defeat the Japanese and drive them out of

The Gurkha statue in London, sculptured by Philip Jackson, and unveiled by Queen Elizabeth II in Horse Guards Avenue, off Whitehall, in December 1997.

Queen Victoria (1819-1901), Empress of India in the days of the Raj, had her own Gurkha trailblazer. Harkabir Thapa ran barefoot up and down the 2,573 ft Glamaig Mountain on the Isle of Skye in the summer of 1899 in the record time of 75 minutes. His record was not broken for 80 years.

His Royal Highness the Duke of Edinburgh who was patron of the British Everest Expedition in 1953, which he described as 'a shining example to all mankind'. The Gurkhas played an enterprising part under the command of Colonel Charles Wylie.

His Royal Highness Prince Charles, Colonel-in-Chief of the Royal Gurkha Rifles in Britain. This relaxed regimental portrait hangs in the reception of the Royal Gurkha Rifles at the Sir John Moore Barracks at Shorncliffe on the outskirts of Folkestone in Kent.

Major Mark Austin, well remembered by his ethnic Gurkha colleagues for hunting wild pigs in the jungle!

Rudyard Kipling (1865-1936) – poet, short story writer and novelist – who wrote mostly about India, including a short story about Gurkha soldiers.

Major Laxmi Bantawa, an elder statesman among ethnic Gurkha officers in Britain, and the first to be given his own voice in a book about the Gurkhas. What a story he has to tell!

Brigadier Peter Pearson, Colonel of the Regiment of Britain's Royal Gurkha Rifles, wherever they are to be found in the world today.

Burma, the biggest volunteer army the world has ever seen rose like a mighty phoenix out of India and loomed large in the Burmese jungles. They came in their colourful turbans, berets and helmets from all the warring tribes of India to join with the Gurkhas, British, North American, Black African, South African, Australasian and Chinese soldiers for a mighty push against the Japs.

As is well known, the Japanese proved to be chief among the world's most sadistic soldiers. We are told in the 2000 edition of the *Bugle & Kukri*, published by the 10th Princess Mary's Own Gurkha Rifles Association, that when Major Lewis William Rose MC was captured by the Japanese, he was tied to a tree with his wounds untended, after being bayoneted in the buttock 'as I lay on the ground'. He was then confronted by 'a Nip officer' who 'spoke impeccable English and said that he had been educated at Winchester! He said that he was going to free my hands and give me back my pistol so I could kill myself, since I had fought honourably until disabled, and that it was dishonourable to be a prisoner. I said I refused to kill myself, since I was a married man and owed it to my wife to survive this war. The officer then said, in that case, he would either shoot me with his pistol or despatch me with his sword: which was it to be? In pain and in a desperate state, I said "If you intend to murder me, you must choose which weapon to use." He was so taken aback by my use of the word "murder" that he spared me.'

One of the Gurkhas' greatest admirers, who became one of their most celebrated officers was Field Marshal the Viscount Slim, who succeeded General Montgomery as Chief of

Imperial General Staff – 'head of Britain's army' as John Masters observed, who was also 'the second and last Knight of the Garter from the Indian Army'.

And why not quote Slim again when he concludes as follows on the subject of war and the 'Forgotten Army': 'No one who saw the 14th Army in action, above all, no one who saw its dead on the field of battle, the black and the white and the brown and the yellow lying together in their indistinguishable blood on the rich soil of Burma, can ever doubt that there is a brotherhood of man; or fail to cry, What *is* Man, that he can give so much for war, so little for peace?'

In the decades that followed the Second World War the Gurkhas were wherever the British were, from Malaysia, South Korea and Borneo to the Falklands, Kosovo and Bosnia. They were also in Hong Kong, policing the border with communist China before the handover of the British Crown Colony.

Because the Gurkhas arrived in the Falklands only a couple of weeks before the war was brought to a speedy conclusion, they were denied the opportunity to get their teeth into things and really live up to their no-nonsense reputation. Even so, young and inexperienced Argentinian soldiers soon wove a perverse fiction out of their short exposure to Gurkha soldiers.

Citing an article by Gabriel García Márquez in *El Espectador* of 3 April 1983, Gould tells us in *Imperial Warriors* that the Argentinian novelist spoke to Argentinian soldiers who survived the war and reported as follows: '"Shouting and beheading," wrote one witness to the merciless butchery, "the rate at which they cut off the heads of our poor boys with their assassins' scimitars was one every seven seconds. In their strange custom, they held the severed head by the hair and cut off the ears."… These beasts were so ferocious that, once the battle for Puerto Argentina [Port Stanley] was finished, they continued killing the English themselves until the English had to shackle them to subdue them.'

Gould cites another article by Márquez, entitled 'The Queen's Gurkhas' and published in *Clarín* on 25 May 1983, in which an Argentinian soldier also reckoned that the Gurkhas 'seemed completely drugged. They even killed one another.' While the British government dismissed these reports as 'pure fairy tales inspired by black propaganda', Gould notes that Márquez, was 'unconvinced, preferring to believe' these bizarre stories.

Meanwhile British soldiers joked that the Argentinians immediately surrendered when Britain sent a Gurkha soldier to confront them with a knife and fork!

It is worth repeating that Colonel Bill Dawson at Gurkha HQ in Britain has explained in an earlier chapter that there is 'no culture among Gurkha soldiers of collecting heads. No cult of headhunting… The Japanese used ritual headhunting as a form of execution, but not the Gurkhas. The Gurkhas are very honourable in their treatment of prisoners' – which is more than can be said for the behaviour of the Argentinian soldiers before Britain's Task Force arrived in the Falklands.

According to Colonel Dawson: 'If Gurkhas ever behaved in the way described by Márquez, the brigade would have been disbanded years ago.'

The mind boggles at the prospect of Argentina's 'poor boys' – the inexperienced but macho young men who were out to spill British and Gurkha blood, while seriously disrespecting the British civilian prisoners they had taken previously, and not expecting any butchery in return – standing around timing their watches to mark the frequency with which Argentinian heads fell, instead of getting on with the business of fighting a war – 'One, two, three, four, five, six, seven… oops! What happened to my head?'

As for the idea of the Gurkhas turning on the British when there were no remaining Argentinians for them to kill, did Márquez really believe this? It would seem that the Gurkhas' blood-and-guts reputation must have gone before them in the Falklands, unnerving and unhinging the macho but deeply immature soldiers who were sent to face them. Perhaps the Argentinian government should have reported this to the United Nations and the War Crimes Tribunal. Perhaps it should have hung its head in shame.

This nonsense about the Gurkhas' behaviour in the Falklands speaks volumes for the psychological grip – the emotional impact – that legend and mythology can have on people's minds, particularly when they find themselves in a nightmarish situation. It also demonstrates how it can be manipulated for political and black propaganda purposes. Clearly, the legend of the Gurkhas is a double-edged sword. On the one hand it can work as a method of psychological warfare in their favour, frightening the enemy out of their wits before a single bullet has been fired and seriously undermining and demoralising them, so that, in this sense, the battle is won before it has begun (because it can work in this way, it can also be promoted for that purpose). But, on the other hand, it can work against the Gurkhas, blackening their name and reputation when they have behaved well, stigmatising them wherever they go, haunting them forever, however much they try to disassociate themselves from the myths about them.

## seven

# PRINCE CHARLES AND THE GURKHAS

The paint has barely dried on the latest military portrait of Prince Charles at the Shorncliffe Barracks of the Royal Gurkha Rifles when I attend a reunion lunch of the now defunct 10th Gurkha Rifles there in June 2002. (The portrait will be unveiled by the Prince the following month.)

The Royal Gurkha Rifles is the UK's only remaining Gurkha regiment – after its amalgamation with three others in 1994 – and it has two battalions, one based in Brunei and the other at Shorncliffe, at Folkestone in Kent. The Shorncliffe Barracks are on a high cliff overlooking the sea, above the mouth of the Channel Tunnel – not, I am told, for strategic military purposes, either with regard to asylum seekers and terrorists coming out of the Tunnel, or future trouble spots in Europe.

Previously the Gurkhas' headquarters in the UK was at

Church Crookham, on the outskirts of Fleet, in Hampshire, where they had been since 1970. In August 2001, when the Gurkhas said farewell to Fleet with a ceremonial march past, Prince Charles, as Colonel-in-Chief of the Regiment, paid his last visit to Gurkha soldiers and their families there, telling them, as reported in the regimental journal, the *Bugle & Kukri*, that he was 'tinged with sadness as your long association with Church Crookham comes to an end' before he joined officers, men and their families at a private barbecue.

Alan Harris, the acting head teacher of the local junior school in Fleet – where a Nepalese garden has been created in the grounds – told the Gurkhas: 'We will miss your humour, your smiles, your cheerfulness and your hard work. But your garden will be with us for years and years and will remind us how beautiful the Gurkha children were.'

Prince Charles's portrait at Shorncliffe is positioned in the reception area, on a wall facing the Delhi Table, which I am told is the hugely famous black-marble tabletop, rescued from Hindo Rao's house at the battle of Delhi Ridge during the Indian Mutiny of 1857–8, when Gurkha soldiers came bravely to the rescue of their British masters. Much blood and water has washed under the bridge since then and here we are today, looking out from the white cliffs across the English Channel – no longer the 'hell corner' that it was during the Battle of Britain days of the Second World War – with the invigorating whiff of seaweed and sea air in our nostrils. It is June, the sun is shining, and the ghosts of the Indian Mutiny and so many other instances of Gurkha heroism have long been laid to rest.

You won't see this portrait of the Prince at the National Portrait Gallery in London, or in the Queen's Gallery at Buckingham Palace, but you will see it here at Shorncliffe, where Charles is looking reassuringly relaxed and content in his rifle-green Gurkha uniform. This is a quiet portrait of a princely man of war, revealing a suitably understated persona: not too spruce or proud, arrogant, regal, prickly or grand, not too ferocious for the demeanour of a military man, but just right for the new millennium and the modern age. Congratulations to the artist, Mark Shields, for such a homely and dignified portrait.

But if the Prince's portrait is barely dry, there is no shortage of real-life brown and white faces at this reunion – both Gurkha and British – on which the paint has dried good and hard for many a year now. These are the fleshy countenances of former men of war, whose fearless exploits over the years have won many a battle in the service of the British Crown and left them smiling their smiles to the very end.

In particular there is the unforgettable, deeply creased and unflinching granite face of the Gurkha officer Rambahadur Limbu VC, square-jawed and firmly set under the broadest of brows. It is a face magnificently and unmistakably full to the brim with character, in which the keen and fearless eyes, missing nothing, scrutinise you closely. Rambahadur, whose dark face, with its bright-brown eyes, is not unlike that of a Red Indian chieftain, has retired to Nepal, but he is visiting today to attend this reunion and to catch up with his son, who is a Gurkha officer at Shorncliffe. This richly dignified face is showing every sign that it is ready, at last, for a well-earned rest after a life of truly astonishing vigour and fearless action, as it contemplates those peaceful twilight years. There are younger versions of this face here today – white as well as brown – that one suspects will also be looking towards welcome retirement when the time comes; and then there are faces, including Limbu's son's face, that are still positively gleaming with youth and have a long way to go yet.

These are the sort of men who well understand Alan Moorhead's observation in the 1999 edition of the *Bugle & Kukri*: 'On the battlefield, the individual vanishes. Men turn with absolute trust to one another. They need one another as they seldom do in time of peace. When the leader takes a daring decision, it should be just the decision all his men would have taken.' But the individuality of these battlefield men is very much in evidence here today. One could not meet a livelier bunch of individuals with the strongest of markedly different characters (no homogenous stuffed shirts or faceless 'men in suits' here). They do not look much like battlefield men. They might pass for golf-club men, and one wonders what it is exactly, other than a possible dislike of golf, that drives such civilised and apparently harmless men to become professional soldiers for the best years of their lives, braving the life-destroying battlefields. (It would be inappropriate to ask such a boorish question at such a happy event as this.)

Rambahadur Limbu's is one of those over-the-hill faces that are never really over the hill at all, because, in fact, here is a man who has actually taken the hill with his own bare hands and tamed it for his own purposes. He is not over the hill. He is the hill! This man with the mountainous heart and a suitably ravaged face to go with it.

This reunion really is a place for the most extraordinary faces, forthright and open, set firm and confident, but very relaxed, most of which are constantly smiling and laughing on this happy occasion. In fact, there are too many delightful and friendly faces for me to describe them all, so no offence, please, to those who are left out. Of course, my description is only one man's subjective and imaginative impression, so it should not be taken too seriously. But it would be remiss of any writer not to get into creative gear and react to these faces, for purely illustrative purposes, as they come at him out of this convivial gathering. For these are facial people and, as one of the British Gurkha officers present puts it to me: 'What you have here is a corner of the Gurkha community, representing a snapshot in time, a portrait of how we all interact with each other, and what makes us tick when we are out of uniform. For a more detailed version of the people present, you would of course need much more time in order to profile them, but as an eye-opener, this little scene is perhaps quite revealing.'

It is, in fact, very revealing. The contrasting faces, attitudes and mannerisms here today reflect the changing times and differences in style between one generation of Gurkha officers and the next. People in different parts of the canvas – at opposite ends maybe – are not unlike the contrasting characters in a painting by, say, Pieter Bruegel or Hieronymus Bosch (one cannot fail to evoke the art of portraiture when interpreting such a richly varied collection). Here there are people from the pre-war days and culture of British India, and then there are other post-war people of the machine age who are both unlike and like those who went before them. There are also present-day people, who started their military careers in the sixties, seventies and eighties, and are different yet again. Temperaments, mentalities and perspectives are different, as is the evolving style and image of the Gurkhas from one era to the next.

There are people who look and behave as though they would have been more comfortable in a much earlier time, and others who look and behave as though it would not have suited them at all. There are those who seem to prefer the *kukri* to the tank and others who do not. Some take an idealised view. Others disagree. There are romantic approvers and disapprovers, all coming together for this gathering. Even people of the same generation do not necessarily conform to type, so it is as well not to generalise too much either about ethnic Gurkhas or Gurkha officers (which is not to say that they will not generally close ranks as and when they think fit!). There are people who will spring to your defence to protect you from the horrors of life in wartime, whom you hardly ever see or think about in peacetime. Each person has his own story to tell and picture to paint, providing insights into the changing relationships between the British Army and its Gurkha officers and soldiers, reflecting the shifting sands and changing colours of time from one generation to the next.

There are some latter-day but old-style Douglas Fairbanks and Stewart Granger faces here (Charles Wylie, Andrew Watt, Nick Worthington, the quietly spoken young Nigel Rowe, the commanding officer in Brunei over for the occasion, Rupert Litherland and the walrus-like Lachhiman Gurung VC all spring to mind), admirably suave smoothies from another and no longer quite fashionable era. There are death-and-glory boys and others who do not fit this image. And then there are much younger and more serious men, with new millennium faces to suit. Life in the Gurkhas is very much a young man's game: you're in at eighteen or nineteen years of age, so that by the time you're forty you've been playing it for more than twenty years. But, young man's game or not, there are plenty of oldies here who show every sign of getting younger by the minute, such is the rejuvenating atmosphere of this happy little gathering.

Charles Wylie is a remarkably youthful colonel for an eighty-two-year-old, even though his health is not what it used to be; a former mountain climber and soldier, he was on John Hunt's 1953 Mount Everest expedition that reached the summit of this previously unconquered mountain. Born in an Indian hill station – his father was also a Gurkha officer – Charles was sent to Marlborough School in Wiltshire, where his housemaster was a keen mountaineer who took him and other boys climbing in Scotland, the Lake District and Wales, as did his uncle, Hugh Crichton-Miller, who also took young Charles climbing in the Swiss Alps.

By the time Charles went to Sandhurst and joined the Gurkhas, he was not exactly lacking in mountaineering experience, so he had something of a headstart, becoming a natural running mate for Gurkha soldiers down from the hills. But the Second World War soon got in the way of such delightful pursuits and it wasn't until Charles returned to his Gurkha regiment in India after the war that he started to climb again, when he found himself posted to Dhamsala – where the Dalai Lama currently lives – with its lovely range of mountains. It was here that Charles learnt the ropes by organising his own lightweight expedition on a 22,000-foot climb up Nilkantha; he also teamed up with fellow Gurkha officer Major Jimmy Roberts on a two-month climbing holiday in the Alps. But then came Indian independence and partition, whereupon Charles went to a British regiment in Malaya, to fight in jungle warfare in the Malayan Emergency against communist insurgents. It was there that he started to climb again and was eventually chosen to join the Himalayan Committee, set up to mount an expedition on Everest. Back in London in the 1950s, the leader of that expedition, John Hunt – an army officer out of Germany with the Sword of Honour from Sandhurst, where he passed out top – invited Charles to join him on the climb. Charles was delighted to accept – and even more delighted when they reached the summit of that famous mountain.

In the 1960s Charles was a founder trustee of the Britain-Nepal Medical Trust in London, which helps to cure tuberculosis and leprosy in Nepal by building clinics and providing medical personnel, expertise and drugs. He tells me: 'The government of Nepal has no money, but we manage to cure about 2,000 TB patients a year in a country in which TB is the biggest killer. The Trust supplements the government's supply of drugs so that there are drugs available year round to all government health institutions – hospitals and health posts.

We have been treating patients there for over thirty years now and our contribution really is vital because the Nepal government's annual supply of drugs is so meagre that it only lasts for two months! We have medical clinics scattered throughout the hills and plains of eastern Nepal, where people come in by human ambulance – one man piggy-backs, with a sick patient on the back of a man who carries him for miles to the nearest clinic. My family has been involved with Nepal for over 100 years. My grandfather was British Resident in Kathmandu for eight years and my father was the Chief Recruiting Officer for the Gurkhas there – both when Nepal was still a closed country and the Gurkha Brigade was of twenty battalions and not just two battalions as now. I was chairman of the Britain-Nepal Society for five years.'

I am inevitably reminded that, when I was growing up in the south-east of England in the 1940s, TB and polio were the biggest killers throughout Britain, and most children were warned by their parents not to drink from cups or bottles shared with others, for fear of contracting TB. So the serious nature of the health problem in Nepal today is not lost on me, or others of my and preceding generations.

Charles Wylie is still very handsome in his remaining years. He has a walking stick in order to get around these days, and is almost deaf, but he is enjoying the reunion for all that, as he drags himself down memory lane with a smile on his face. He is a man from the ghostly Gurkha past, in stark contrast to so many of his younger counterparts today, and he is currently writing a book about the Gurkhas.

This is a shirt-and-tie reunion at which the white British

officers, accompanied by their wives, are mostly wearing lounge suits, and the ethnic Gurkha officers, accompanied by their sari-clad wives, are wearing blazers or sports jackets (the blazers are navy blue or an attractive rifle green).

A younger ethnic Gurkha officer, looking more Mongolian or Chinese than Indian, is telling me that he regards the British as the best soldiers in the world, the bravest of the brave, which is why he and his kind respect them so much and consider it a privilege and an honour to fight alongside them. He is telling me this in a sincere, impassive, matter-of-fact way, not seeking to flatter or gild the lily (Gurkhas never appear to do so). He and his Gurkha colleagues are also explaining to me that most of their race is of Mongolian rather than Indian origin, although they cannot deny that there is some intermingling of Indian blood as well. Most of the Gurkhas are short and stocky and some, like Rambahadur Limbu, are barrel-chested. Others are lean and slim but very muscular. Without exception they are all very polite, tolerant and respectful, without being obsequious, awkward or apprehensive in any way, and they are very much at ease and self-confident in the company of their white counterparts.

Fifty-four-year-old Brigadier Peter Pearson CBE – big chief of the Royal Gurkha Rifles wherever they are to be found in the world – is also short and stocky. He is an ex-10th Gurkha officer, with short-cropped, bushy hair, and is bright-eyed and bushy-tailed, with a face that is mischievous and somewhat gentle and boyish for a man who has been in the Gurkhas for twenty-eight years; his large, round face is also a kindly one. He was the last commanding officer of the

Gurkhas in Hong Kong, before the handover of the Crown Colony to the Chinese, but now he is being promoted to major general in order to go to Bosnia before the end of summer as deputy commander of operations there.

Prince Charles last visited Brigadier Pearson and his Gurkha regiment in Hong Kong in November 1994, when he took the salute at the Gurkha recruits' final passing-out parade before the Crown Colony's depot was transferred lock, stock and barrel to Fleet the following month. In 1995 the regiment proceeded to train Gurkhas in the UK for the first time in their long and distinguished history. (As mentioned in the previous chapter, two years earlier Her Majesty the Queen unveiled a statue of a Gurkha soldier in London's Horse Guards Avenue, so the ground had been prepared and the welcoming mat had been put out for the Gurkhas in no uncertain way.)

Peter Pearson is telling me that the copyright of the colour print of Prince Charles's portrait – the Prince has given his permission to the artist to include it in his catalogue – is the property of the Royal Gurkha Rifles at Shorncliffe, so I will have to apply formally to the regiment in order to use it in my book. The brigadier's wife, Francesca, says that her husband will be going to Kosovo for only one year, so she will not be accompanying him this time.

Another officer is remarking that Peter Pearson was 'a long-haired hippy when he went up to Sandhurst in the swinging sixties, a new breed of Gurkha officer'. He explains that he is 'not in the standard mould of a soldier, much warmer and more approachable'.

Lieutenant Colonel Ian Thomas, the commanding officer at Shorncliffe, who read history at Oxford, is watching a video of a recent holiday visit of British officers and their families to Nepal, shown by colonels Bicket and Bill Dawson, and Thomas has the face of a man who is somewhat shy and faintly amused by it all (he is probably neither of these things, but that's how he seems to me today). But he says, seriously enough, that he doesn't think much of the military action paintings that are hanging on the walls at Shorncliffe and show Gurkhas in battle. He thinks they are passable, but nothing more than that. The other portraits are better, he says, among which is a very young Duke of Edinburgh. Well, that's as may be, but I am glad that these action paintings are hanging on the walls, because they do evoke the Gurkha past, so they are appropriate in this military context, and Shorncliffe is not supposed to be an art gallery. It is well served, it seems to me, by its paintings.

This is very much a cosy, family affair. I'm the only man present who is not a Gurkha officer and I am tolerated, with cheerful good humour, because of the book that I am writing. In the company of so many extremely capable men of war, past and present, whose reputation has long gone before them, I am reminded of Auchinleck's remark, quoted by Philip Warner in his book *Auchinleck – The Lonely Soldier*: 'From the first moment of joining, the recruit is taught – if he does not already believe it – that the regular services are a breed apart. They have chosen a way of life and taken an oath binding them to its tenets. They will defend their civilian countrymen, but they cannot help but feel superior to them.'

As a civilian whose only claim to military action is modest – national service from 1959 to 1961 with the Royal Corps of Signals in Cyprus, where I was attached to the Turkish Army for a while, at the tail end of the war against Greek Cypriot terrorists – I certainly feel a bit like a new recruit today, surrounded by a famously superior breed that is indeed apart from the rest of us. And while there is nothing in the outward appearance of these unassuming and restrained Gurkha people and their white British officers to suggest that they do actually feel superior, I wouldn't for one moment be surprised (or doubt) that they do, and I certainly do not begrudge them their superiority, God help them. These rugged, cordial people have a long tradition of facing up to the kind of terrors and cruel hardships that most people would run away from at the drop of a hat, so it seems to me that they are perfectly entitled to their quiet superiority. They probably are, inescapably, Auchinleck's breed apart, and in a society in which virtually every profession feels superior to others – think of lawyers, judges, surgeons, intellectuals and academics, for a start – why should they not feel superior, if that's what they need to feel? It doesn't bother me – or, I hope, the readers of this book. War is a gruesome and brutalising business, but I am relieved to say that none of these people strike me as being brutalised by their experiences. How they do it is anybody's guess.

I am very encouraged by the way in which white British officers and their ethnic Gurkha counterparts greet each other with handshakes and the occasional bear hug. They seem genuinely pleased to see each other and delighted to be in one another's company, as they talk among themselves in

Gurkhali. Yes, they are talking Gurkhali, these white British officers, and the Gurkhas really appreciate it. Nowhere else in Europe or the UK is so much Gurkhali (or perhaps any other foreign language in the UK for that matter) being spoken under one roof. So who dares to say that the British cannot speak foreign tongues? There are dozens of white British officers here, young and old, speaking a foreign language like natives. With their mastery of the basics of Gurkhali, they put a good number of Britain's export salesmen and businessmen to shame. There is a good, informal approach and conversational exchange in this tongue between the chattering military classes of East and West. Brigadier Pearson says that it's 'not difficult' to learn Gurkhali.

Major Mark Austin – at thirty-seven, young enough to be my son – is over six feet tall and has a long and somewhat studious face. He tells me that the Gurkhali being spoken is a specially adapted, military form of Nepali. But it clearly works like a charm with the Gurkhas and their wives. Even some of the British officers' wives are able to offer a few complimentary sentences, as they point with their v-shaped hands to Gurkha ladies and bow their heads in traditional style. There is an unmistakable cut-glass elegance about this little social gathering that would not be misplaced at a Buckingham Palace garden party. Predictably, there are some perfectly splendid, slow-moving British officers here today, in their twilight years (almost but not quite in their dotage), but they too are fast-tongued when it comes to speaking Gurkhali. Some of them left the regiment sixty years ago, yet they are still speaking the language. Unlike their bodies, their Gurkhali has not gone to rust over the decades (there are also some marvellous old ethnic Gurkha officers who, likewise, can still speak English). Young and middle-aged British officers – some left the regiment about twenty years ago, others are still in it – are comfortably chatting in Gurkhali to Gurkhas, obviously delighted to be able to speak the language.

Elderly Gurkha officer Major Nick Carter – whose wife Jill sketches and has produced with him a little guidebook about Majorcan monasteries, following a holiday on the island, where their son edits a local English-language newspaper – is still able to speak Gurkhali. He is one of those regimental faces on whom the paint has long dried, and he is telling me that he tours the UK interpreting for Nepalese asylum seekers who have fled to Britain. He has an amusing and sad story to tell about a Nepalese immigrant called Kamal at Gravesend police station who told him: 'I could never go back to Nepal, as I'm an active member of the Maoist Party… The Police will be after me … so I am coming to England.' It is Maoist rebels, of course, that the Gurkhas have fought in their time, and who to this day attack retired Gurkha veterans when they return to Nepal, to see if they can relieve the old soldiers of their pensions! It is the wild boys from the poverty-stricken Nepalese hills – hardened young men – who are joining the Maoist terror gangs now that the British Army is not recruiting them in great numbers, as once it did. Irony, irony, irony! I think I'll have another drink.

As Nick has written in an article entitled 'The Asylum Racket – A Cautionary Tale' in the 2002 edition of the *Bugle & Kukri*: 'It is well known that this party creates mayhem in

Nepal. They are well armed, further their aims by terrorism, think nothing of murder and arson, and in particular rob returning soldiers of their pension money. Just one more terrorist in our midst. Enough said.'

Nick lives in Ramsgate and, when he arrived at Gravesend police station to interview his Nepalese gentleman, there was 'an Afghan' who was 'first in the queue'. In his article Nick observes: 'An Afghan? Didn't they fight three wars against us while demonstrating the utmost barbarism and treachery? The "In Memoriam" tablets in Rochester Cathedral just down the road are filled with the names of our men killed by them.'

In another article in the same magazine, Nick is photographed in Majorca with the Welsh singer and former *Goon Show* entertainer Harry Secombe, who is doing an episode of *Songs of Praise* for BBC television there, and in that piece Nick quotes Dr Johnson – 'every man thinks meanly of himself for not having been a soldier' – and he reports that 'El Gordo, the fat one' was 'proud of having been a soldier' and amused to have 'become known as Joker Sahib' after he met the Gurkhas at a Royal Tournament.

Like so many other Gurkha officers of his generation here today, Major Nick Carter is one of a dying breed, and there is, as always, a new breed following swiftly in their wake, one of whom is forty-five-year-old Major Laxmi Bantawa, an elder statesmen among serving Gurkha officers. A member of the Queen's Gurkhas, he has a youthful, smiling, open and welcoming face. He is telling Mark Austin: 'I am happy to see that you have not lost your Gurkhali. The language is always maintained by those who speak it from the heart.'

This is true of all languages, of course, and there is no shortage of white British officers here today who speak it from the heart. They really do, as their hearts go out to their Gurkha friends and their wives, with whom they are about to sit down and eat a delicious Gurkha curry in the officers' mess, washed down with lashings of red and white wine (so far Gurkha officers have been drinking fistfuls of beer in king-size silver goblets, while the ladies have been sipping at long glasses of gin and tonic).

Major Austin is telling me that all career-minded white Gurkha officers, who are in for the long haul, are required to take Gurkhali seriously. While 'look-see' officers who are just on attachment for a couple of years are also required to speak the language, they may not take it seriously if they decide not to stay on. But permanent officers must certainly complete the language course satisfactorily, if not with distinction, then with a good enough pass mark to be able to converse with their Gurkha soldiers and officers. And they must keep up to speed with the language. They can fail the course as many times as it takes, but they must return to it time and again until they have got the hang of the language and passed the course, and in addition to their classroom studies they can be tutored for a couple of hours every evening by English-speaking Gurkhas. That's why there are so many Gurkhali-speaking white British officers. If they fail first or second time, the system does not wash its hands of them – as the British education and academic systems do when foreign-language students fail – nor does it give them a great inferiority complex on account of it. It simply hauls them back and says try again until you get it right. Although there is not the same need to speak Gurkhali as there used to be in the old days, the language requirement remains an important part of a British officer's training, as does the requirement to learn about Gurkha culture and history.

According to Colonel Dawson: 'You are useless until you speak the language. You cannot command a section or platoon unless you do.'

But there are two reasons why there is not the same need for Gurkhali as before. To begin with, Britain's Gurkha army is very much smaller than it used to be, so there are fewer Gurkhas in the ranks, with whom British officers must communicate. As a result, British officers are not as close to as many men as before, now that the Empire is long gone and there is far less territory to be patrolled and policed by Gurkhas, many of whom had little or no knowledge of English in those days. Secondly, many more Gurkha recruits are a lot better educated these days, so they are much more fluent in English than their Gurkha predecessors, so a higher proportion of the overall intake are English-speaking. Even so, the tradition remains for British officers to speak Gurkhali if they intend to become a permanent fixture, and most British officers I met, not only love speaking the language, but also love going to Nepal at every opportunity. Speaking Gurkhali is seen as essential to the continuing ethos and spirit of the regiment, which is why a Gurkha officer whose heart is not in acquiring Gurkhali is not going to make it as a Gurkha officer.

But today it's not just a matter of speaking the language from the heart. British hearts have gone out to their ethnic

Gurkhas to the tune of £450,000 – raised by the 10th Gurkha Rifle Association by auctioning a surfeit of regimental silver, thirty lots, that accrued after the recent amalgamation of four regiments into one. Bids in sealed envelopes have been arriving for weeks, from all over the country, for silver trophies, tableware and dinner sets, in order to raise much-needed money for Gurkha community projects in Nepal – which, as everybody knows, is a desperately poor country. The financial proceeds are to be generously handed over to Gurkha communities that have served the British so loyally over so many years. There has been a wholehearted response from British Gurkha officers and their families, and there are still a few remaining items to be sold off today, including a selection of the famous and doubtless illegal *kukri* (so I buy one for £50).

There is such a fine feeling of brotherhood and goodwill, such a strong sense of family between white-skinned British officers and brown-skinned Gurkha officers and their respective families. There is no mistaking it. The atmosphere is fully alive with it, as wrinkled and unwrinkled soldiers and former soldiers – crumblies and smoothies – recapture their past together while their wives show every sign of likewise enjoying the occasion.

A perceptive observer could not fail to notice at this gathering that we are all coated and decorated with life's colouring matter, which makes a picture of our faces and our lives. I have touched on this metaphor from painting before and I mention it again simply to let today's colours and atmosphere sink in to the reader's consciousness, as they have sunk into mine.

There are people at this gathering who are fashioned and project themselves more vividly, more colourfully, than others and that is because their military experience has been more vivid than others (perhaps with more military decorations than others, with more suffering and heroism than others, but not necessarily so); whilst there are, very likely, some who will become vivid in the fullness of time, as life paints them into and out of corners, or on and off battlefields somewhere or other in this world of endless battles of one kind or another. There are understated and overstated people here, imaginative and unimaginative people, memorable and not so memorable faces – masks? – of all kinds, and they are all speaking with one voice, certainly, but from a widely differing and contrasting background of experiences. The Falklands, Bosnia, Burma, latter-day India, the Himalayas, Japanese prisoner-of-war camps, aristocratic backgrounds, middle and lower-middle-class backgrounds – but no working-class that I can see – and different racial origins are all very different experiences that have coloured these people, even though they are of the same Gurkha tribe.

And there are white Gurkha officers here who are as different, in their way, as the original Gorkha tribes of Limbus, Gurungs, Rais and Magars. There are paternalistic John Masters types and those who are decidedly not of that type at all, and there do not appear to be any arrogant or egotistical types such as one certainly finds at social gatherings of some other professions that I could mention (as it happens, I am about to be reminded of this by Colonel Bill Dawson). There are some white Gurkha officers who feel that

I should not be in attendance and others who are pleased to see me. There is one who says that journalists 'have never been my favourite people' (bless him, a lot of people say the same of soldiers) and there is another who has described me as 'a real persistent pain' because I have asked too many questions. And there is one who says that he likes talking to journalists 'for a broader view'.

All of these people are painted differently by their experience of life. The way that they perceive others is made up of subtle shades of colouring not immediately visible to the human eye. There is an inescapable analogy between painting and impressionistic writing that seems to work particularly well for military men, whose blood-and-guts exploits require them to be depicted, once in a while, in a way that rises above the level of gun smoke. They are all 'persona faces', to quote my old friend Colonel John Liveing of Henley-upon-Thames.

There is something magnificent and unknowable about the relationship between life and art, about never really knowing how the latter is going to work out or show up (but not being able to resist it for all that). The portrait of Prince Charles in the reception area is not liked by all – somebody has even suggested that the prince isn't too keen on it himself – but its magic for me is that it has captured him differently (and appropriately) for a change, so perhaps his mood was very different when he sat for it, or perhaps the artist perceived him in a light different from the customary light that is shed on such paintings.

Colonel Bill Dawson, an elder officer with a fresh and calm face, a cuddly bear of a man with an excellent sense of humour and a reputation for being lively, outspoken, upfront, straight and all heart – or 'full on' as a younger officer expressed it to me – tells me that he finds the *Daily Mirror*'s accusations of racism among white officers towards ethnic Gurkhas 'deeply offensive'. And on the evidence of this reunion lunch one can well understand why he feels this way. There seems to be no racial bias, deference, disharmony or displeasure on either the Gurkha or the British side. The two races appear to be very comfortable with, and respectful of, each other, very happy and content to be together.

Certainly, the self-confident ethnic Gurkha officers and their wives look as though they are very much at home and part of the family, and not at all apprehensive, awkward, humbled or fearful of upsetting their white counterparts in any way. That's how they look, these proud and smiling gutsy Gurkhas. They do not strike one as the kind of people who hide their emotions for fear of upsetting their white officers, who, likewise, do not come over as the least bit condescending or racist in their warm-hearted responses to their Gurkha friends. Everybody looks as though they are having a good time, and are pleased with one another, and the Gurkhas have a reputation for letting it be known, in no uncertain manner, when they are displeased. Nobody here seems to have a seriously racist bone in his or her body. There is nothing but good vibes here, regardless of race – a warm and affectionate glow that is, as Major Laxmi would say, from the heart – so one can readily understand why Colonel Dawson is so offended by the *Daily Mirror* (if the 'political' legislation governing the British Army's relationship with its Gurkha soldiers is racist, that is something else, but one cannot blame soldiers for this), and Major Laxmi Bantawa has promised me an interview on this and other subjects on another day (see Chapter 10).

Bill Dawson was with the Gurkhas in the Falklands when Britain invaded and took back the island from Argentina, as was Gurkha Major (QGO) Rambahadur Rai. When Gurkha soldiers went on a goose hunt at Goose Green, to hunt game instead of Argentinians, because they were short of food, Rai quipped: 'If they carry on at this rate, we shall have to call it Just Green in future.'

Dawson tells me that: 'Pre-war there was a different ethos to that which we have today, with more paternalism perhaps, such as you find in John Masters' early books, but a lot of that sort of paternalism went out after the Second World War. When I joined in the sixties there was not the same sort of rigorous screening of officers as previously, or perhaps the same sort of desire to get in, but we felt that we were joining an elite – the cream of the British Army – but there was no trace of the paternalism of the Masters era. What there was instead was great camaraderie, which is just as well, because people don't die for Queen and Country any more, if they ever did, but they do die for each other, for their peer group and their regiment. They don't want to let their friends down by being cowardly or feeble. It's extraordinary what people will do for each other, how brave they can be for one another. And not just soldiers. In the 1960s, Gurkha wives in saris guarded beaches in Malaya with Bren guns while their men were out fighting in the jungle. They guarded the beaches to deter Indonesians from landing in Malaya, in the absence of

their husbands, and the wives were happy to do this'
(Imagining the sari-clad wives who are here today, with Bren
guns in their hands, puts them in an interesting new light –
what a painting that would make for the officers mess.)

One could add that, in an age of anti-heroism, in which, by
common consent, few causes are considered worth dying for
any more, it is rare indeed to find any people at all who are
prepared to die either to protect us from the horrors of this
world, or far less to escape cowardice.

Colonel Dawson is the Brigade Secretary and he is one of
the British officers who went straight to officer cadet school
instead of going to university, after he completed his A levels
at Bromsgrove, a minor public school in the Midlands where
his father, who had no military experience himself, had been
the chief scientist and engineer of a chemical company. He
says: 'The Gurkhas have this fearsome reputation but they are
the most gentle people – always providing you don't wind
them up too much, or get them too angry.' He tells me that
today's Gurkhas have much more contact with and exposure
to white British officers and communities. 'I wonder what the
average well-mannered Gurkha thinks of Europeans now that
he sees them at football matches?' he asks.

Another white Gurkha officer is telling me that, before the
Second World War, British Gurkha officers and their white
wives, many of whom are here today – who were in India and
elsewhere in the colonies – were 'well educated and well
mannered, tolerant and good to their Gurkha soldiers. They
might have been an upper-class oddity, perhaps, or even
arrogant, but they were clever with it, and when what is left of

them these days sets eyes on the oiks and yobs that we have in Britain, they think, Jesus wept, what have we here? These officers did a good job and they appealed to Gurkhas as leaders of men.'

Major Laxmi Bantawa recalls how, when he served with Major Mark Austin, they were digging pits in the jungle to catch wild pigs for their dinner, camouflaging the pits so that the pigs would fall into them. Unfortunately for Mark, he forgot where one of the pits was and fell into it himself. This caused Laxmi and his Gurkhas to go into predictable hoots of laughter and they still laugh about it whenever they are reminded of Mark. A white British officer falling into a disguised pit that he has instructed his Gurkha soldiers to dig and to camouflage is quite amusing. The thing about ethnic Gurkhas and their British officers is that they know how to laugh at themselves. They enjoy banana-skin humour.

Colonel Dawson explains to me that it was much more difficult for British officers to get into the Gurkhas in the days of the British Imperial Army: 'In those days they took only the top five per cent of officers coming out of Sandhurst. Only the cream of the officer class, not just for the Gurkhas, but for all Indian Army regiments, because so many British officers wanted to go to India, where you could live on your pay. But, since then, we have had to lower our standards – we must have done otherwise I wouldn't have got in! – and we recruit from the top twenty or thirty per cent at Sandhurst.' (Among those who did not gain high enough grades at Sandhurst to get into the Imperial Army in India was Britain's war hero Field Marshal Montgomery, as we are reminded in Chapter 5 of this book.)

Even so, Brigadier Pearson says that, with the British Paras, the Gurkhas remain the most glamorous and sought-after regiment for British officers, no doubt on account of their high profile in the media and their enduring mystique. He has previously explained, before my arrival today, that British Gurkha officers are 'a thoroughly mixed bunch, who come from all sorts of educational and social backgrounds. What is important to the selection board is that the officer will fit in and *be beneficial to our soldiers*.'

Being beneficial to Gurkha soldiers is what it's all about – not the other way round – and Pearson reckons: 'At Sandhurst, an officer will have shown enthusiasm for service with Gurkha soldiers and an understanding of what that service will entail. He will also be a good soldier. Thus you will find the Eton-educated alongside those who have lived much of their life in Africa and others who may have started life as a soldier in another part of the British Army. The majority of officers at Sandhurst – some eighty to ninety per cent, I believe – are university entrants. So most of our officers nowadays are university educated. However, we have recently taken a young man who did not go to university and another who transferred from the ranks of a Guards regiment. From this you will understand that educational achievement and social background are not at the top of the list of important characteristics of our potential officer recruits.'

Colonel Dawson explains: 'Whilst some eighty-five to ninety per cent of our officers have university degrees these days, they must still get into Sandhurst, which is not easy, since we only have seven or eight places per year for the

Royal Gurkha Rifles and we get about 100 officers competing for these places annually. Most of them have no previous Gurkha connections or backgrounds. We finally select during the twenty-first or twenty-second week at Sandhurst, when we say, "yes, they're in the top one-third and are doing well" and when our Gurkha rep at the college tells us that the officers in question are likely to be psychologically compatible with our Gurkhas.

'We do not tolerate any arrogant, petulant or egotistical types, or people who are always trying to prove how clever they are. We are looking for competent officers who know their trade and can do the business, but the major factor is compatibility with our Gurkha ethos – which is tolerance, a sense of humour, patience and a keen interest in the Gurkhas and their culture. We are not interested in religious bigots or anyone who does not have the patience to work with sometimes obtuse Nepalis. We are looking for enthusiastic types who are dead honest. Gurkhas must believe that their officers are straight men and that there is no nepotism in the regiment. This is because they have seen too much corrupt nepotism in their own country. If you are dishonest with a Gurkha and make promises you cannot keep, your name is mud, as with any other soldier. We have three selection boards at Sandhurst every year and they only take two or three officers per board – six or seven in total per annum, so a lot of applicants are culled. Those that get through embark on an initial three-year short service commission, during which time, if they don't make the grade, or their attitude is wrong, they go. But, once bitten by the Gurkha bug, most want to stay and make it with us in style. Our recruitment in Nepal is no less rigorous, as it is in this country. Gurkhas must be mentally and physically tough and fit. We have 23,000 Nepalis competing for only 230 places every year, so we set rigid physical and IQ tests.'

Major Mark Austin is another of the Sandhurst officers who was not university educated. Born in 1964 in Sri Lanka, where his father was a banker with the Hong Kong & Shanghai Bank, and his mother a midwife nurse, he was brought up in a colonial environment and a home that regularly received Asian and Japanese business people and other guests. His father – who was not a military man, never having served in the army – could speak Japanese, having worked in Tokyo, and as one might expect, Mark was exposed from a young age to Asians of all sorts, not least at the Alice Smith primary day school in Kuala Lumpur. After seeing a Gurkha military parade in that city, he kept a souvenir *kukri* on his bedroom wall and, when his parents retired to England, Mark attended the Truro Cathedral School in Cornwall, where he got it into his head that he would like to return to the Far East as an officer in a Gurkha regiment. So, after A levels, he applied to Sandhurst instead of going to university, and was accepted, not least because of his colonial background with its multi-cultural grasp of things in that part of the world. He could demonstrate knowledge not only of the Gurkhas but also of other Asian races.

He tells me: 'There were a lot of colonials when first I arrived at the Brigade of Gurkhas in 1984 – about half the intake – most of whom were white Kenyans, South Africans,

New Zealanders and Australians. There was also a Gurkha demonstration company at Sandhurst, where real Gurkhas fulfilled the role of the enemy on exercises and also demonstrated platoon attacks to us, so we had an instant appreciation of their impressive abilities as soldiers. The reason why the Gurkhas have become a high-profile glamour regiment currently, with many more officers wanting to join them than before, is because – together with the Paras – they have been the first into trouble spots such as Bosnia, Kosovo, Sierra Leone, East Timor, the Gulf War and the Falklands – not to mention Sudan, Eritrea, Burundi, Liberia, the Congo and the Great Lakes of Africa – so their media profile has been very high in recent years, which is why ambitious young officers who are looking for quick action, medals and promotion are obviously attracted to regiments that are more active in battle than others.

'We have a new parachute air assault brigade and a commando brigade, both capable of being used independently, so we have plenty of swank for men of action. But when I joined the Gurkhas, they were relatively inactive, based in Hong Kong and/or Brunei, where not much was happening, so not too many officers wanted to sit out their careers in a sleepy Gurkha regiment where there was not the same opportunity to do anything exciting or draw blood as there is in Gurkha regiments today.

'Things have changed because, back in the eighties, most warfare was with the armoured regiments, so you needed experience in heavy armour to get ahead as an officer. But with the withdrawal and break-up of the British Army of the

Rhine, there was a switch to light armoured, sporadic derring-do warfare in different parts of the world, and this is where the Paras, Commandos and Gurkhas come into their own. So they were suddenly flavour of the month with keen young officers – thrusting young blades wanting to make a name for themselves.

'As for me, I had a different agenda, with no lofty career ambitions. I went to Sandhurst to get into the Gurkhas full stop. I didn't want to do anything else and it didn't bother me that I might never be seen or heard of again if I went to Hong Kong or Brunei, a part of the world that I loved. I didn't want to go in any other direction. I just wanted to do a useful job in the Far East. Of my 1984 Sandhurst intake of 250, only about four or five officers went into the Gurkhas. But now they are falling over themselves to get into the regiment.'

Mark Austin had to leave the Gurkhas early on, when he got a muscular disease, and these days he is in charge of in-house training at the Halifax Bank of Scotland. But he says that he will always miss the Gurkhas and regrets 'not being able to bring my children up in that environment'.

Clearly, there is a danger of some white officers wanting to join the Gurkhas for the wrong reasons, for the glamour only, and the selection board does its best to separate the glamour pusses from the men, by expecting applicants to know a fair amount about the Gurkhas in advance, and to have a good and convincing reason for wanting to join the regiment. If they have taken the bother to read some Gurkha history and/or to visit Nepal – if they already know something about the culture and customs (which they will later have to study in depth) and if they like the food – then they stand a better chance than those who do not. And if they have any O or A levels to suggest linguistic aptitude when it comes to learning Gurkhali, so much the better (not that Mark Austin had any such qualifications, yet he still managed to get a good mark in Gurkhali). I am told that a young man who has not got more than just a couple of A levels can still get into Sandhurst, along with the majority who have university degrees. There are Gurkha officers here today who have done just that, one with A levels in Geography and History, another with Physics and Chemistry.

An ethnic Gurkha officer is telling me that he much prefers British officers with a colonial background, or Asian experience, especially if they understand something of the customs, culture and religions of his part of the world, and enjoy the spicy food. He finds such officers more internationally minded. I say that I would join up for the food alone and he laughs at this.

I also tell him that during my national service I was attached – suddenly and unexpectedly, without warning or any preparation – to the Turkish Army in Cyprus in the late fifties and early sixties. There, in the absence of any induction into the subtleties of Turkish culture, temperament, military ethos or language, I and a handful of other British soldiers had to muddle through as best we could, working things out as we went along, with brutal and terrible Turks from the slums of Turkey, who did not give us an easy ride, even though we were on the same side in our war against Greek Cypriot terrorists. Among the Turks there was deep mistrust of the British and fierce and undisciplined rivalry towards them. As we Brits did our best not to be intimidated by the Turks, or think the worst of them, since they were supposed to be our allies, there was culture shock, and a clash of cultures (and, ahem, fists) on a daily basis, as British signalmen and teleprinter operators worked with English-speaking Turkish officers to give them a signals facility that their own men were either too thick or too unaccustomed to set up for themselves. How ironic that our mysterious Turkish allies, who were expected to be our friends, turned out to be just as hostile as, if not worse than, our Greek Cypriot enemies! Strange bedfellows indeed, dismissive and distrustful of each other, racist towards one another, as we pulled together, but in opposite directions. Not natural running mates. If the Brits drilled at six in the morning, the Turks drilled at five. If the Brits ran five miles in the heat every day, the Turks ran ten in their pathetic attempts to remind us that anything we could do, they could do better. We were not happy bunnies, though happily for the minority of Brits, surrounded by so many unco-operative and potentially violent Turkish allies, they were, as it turned out, quite good with their fists. (It must have been all that compulsory boxing at school in the forties and fifties!)

To give this story some historical perspective, we were among 30,000 British troops sent to contain Greek Cypriot terrorists under General Grivas, the terrorist leader in Cyprus, where the Turkish Army currently has 30,000 troops in order to hold its half of the island. When the British finally pulled out, United Nations put in some 2,500 peace-keeping troops in 1964, but they could not keep out either the Greek army of occupation under the fascist generals (when the terrorist Nicos Sampson replaced Archbishop Makarios), or the 10,000-strong Turkish army of invasion that swiftly followed and grew in strength, remaining there to this day on a divided island with its own 'Berlin Wall'.

Compared to the 'poor bloody infantry', life in an army corps is relatively soft (more like the RAF), and this suited us just fine in the Royal Corps of Signals, where we had to use our brain cells most of the time (scoring upwards of 120 in IQ tests in order to get in and then learning and regularly practising our trade). Even so, we were roughed up pretty badly by Guards sergeants during basic training at Catterick Camp on the Yorkshire Moors, which was a real pain, and this came in handy when we suddenly found ourselves up against dangerous terrorists and hostile and brutal Turkish allies on the eastern Mediterranean island of the 'goddess of love'. Combat training in ice, snow and fog on the windswept Yorkshire moors was no picnic and, if that didn't make a man of you, then the ferocious and physically powerful Guards sergeants certainly would, by the time they were through with you. I recall that my squad at Catterick had a Welsh Guards sergeant, who made our lives hell, and that we really pleased him when we won the 'golden pace stick' for being the top squad. I also remember his last smiling words to me, which were something like: 'You're the only person I have ever met who can tell a man to his face that he is a bastard, whilst making it appear, by your choice of words, that you are actually complimenting him – other than that, you're not such a bad soldier, I suppose.' And that wasn't a bad assessment of me as a soldier, I suppose – 'not bad,' but certainly not especially good.

It is against this unspectacular background of military experience that I find myself writing this book, and I suppose that it helps, when talking to so many military men in the process, to at least have been 'not bad' as a soldier, if only for a couple of years. It certainly helped me to get on to their wavelength. (It also helps to be 'a real persistent pain'.)

In those days, the last thing that reluctant national servicemen were trying to be, were particularly good soldiers. On the contrary, they could not wait for demob and the advent of the swinging sixties (just visible round the corner), and if they had any brains they wanted to use them in a corps such as Signals, Intelligence, Education, that sort of thing. They did not at all want to put their life on the line for some political argument between historically prejudiced Greek and Turkish Cypriots, which they felt was nothing to do with them, but everything to do with the British politicians who had sent them there, and they probably agreed with almost everyone else in British society that there were almost no remaining causes worth dying for. Even so, national service was responsible for the making of a great many reluctant teenagers into men, and there can be no doubt that it would not harm some of the more outrageous and implausible specimens of pathetic early manhood walking the streets of Britain today.

As anyone who has served in the armed forces must surely know, when it comes to fighting and/or killing, it takes mental as well as physical strength and stamina to be shot at – to kill or not to be killed – and to put one's life on the line, and it may very well take emotional insensitivity and nerves of steel too. As for spiritual strength – that inner faith that gets people through their darkest hours – that also has a part to play. So, too, has arrogance. There are also questions of morality and self-belief. But none of this is an attractive subject to the civilised peacetime world. However, the qualities I'm talking about can help to save that world when its civilisation and freedoms are threatened. Some people have more physical than mental strength. Others have more emotional insensitivity and stronger nerves than spiritual inner faith. And some have no morality or arrogance at all. But, whatever the mix, it all comes tumbling out, like skeletons out of the cupboard, when men go to war.

A white Gurkha officer is telling me that, when he served with ethnic Gurkhas, a British officer who wanted to get the best out of them had to give them time to cook a good curry – two hours – and then more time to eat it properly, perhaps another hour at least. He says that the Gurkha attitude to white British officers was that, if they led by example (which is what ethnic Gurkhas do), and looked after their men (with a white officer not being afraid to use his influence with his superiors in the hierarchy), then Gurkha soldiers would reciprocate by looking after their white officers.

According to Major Austin: 'You don't get this in the Paras, for example. I was on attachment to the Paras for a while, where the men were very hard and their attitude was equally hard. They took the view that all officers were on their own and could not look to their men to look after them.

On the contrary, they sometimes went out of their way to play practical jokes on their officers and to prove that they were not as hard as the ordinary soldiers who served with them in the ranks, and they were highly amused if this proved to be the case. Nor did the Paras care much for fussing around about food and they mistakenly believe that Gurkhas who greet their officers – after a hard day out on an gruelling exercise or in battle – with a cup of tea, or a decent meal, are being obsequious, which is not the case at all. Gurkha hard men don't know how to be obsequious, but they do know how to be caring and civilised, how to look after those who look after them.

'The ethos and atmosphere in a Gurkha regiment is very different from that in a cold-blooded parachute regiment, where there is not the same warmth. The Paras are extremely professional and nobody can take that away from them. They like to perpetuate that image, which is very important to them. They never forget it. They must always be the hardest at drinking and fighting, whatever. Gurkha soldiers watch Paras getting completely paralytic and wonder why they get into that state. It's where the Paras come from, of course, and it's a very big culture difference.'

Colonel Dawson worked with the Paras and he says: 'In the Paras contempt seems to be a part of the ethos, not just for the enemy, but for any authority other than their own. They don't seem to accept that the rest of the army has much of a part to play. Paras are incredibly fit, tough guys, head-down shock troops who will knock out the enemy very efficiently. The British Para sets out to be the roughest, toughest, meanest bastard on the block, nastier than anybody else, killing more people than anybody else, and doing more press-ups than anybody else. His attitude is, "I can do forty press-ups on one arm while pissed and with a rock tied to my willie!" That's your British Para. He is, however, a very effective soldier. Whilst there is little that Paras can do that our Gurkha soldiers cannot, it is true that the Paras generally do it a lot faster than most other soldiers. The Paras were, of course, magnificent on the Falklands, but you must remember that the Gurkhas produced two wartime parachute battalions – 153 and 154 – under Field Marshal Slim, after they retreated from Burma, with just 300 surviving troops of the 700 they started with.'

Brigadier Pearson takes the view that his Gurkha soldiers are 'very different from Paras, Commandos and the SAS' because the Gurkhas are 'much more self-disciplined and contained'. Gurkhas serving in today's Indian rather than the British Army are, he says, 'the same as those in the UK – highly regarded'. He thinks that Gurkha soldiers are 'very similar' to Japanese soldiers, 'save for the fanaticism' of the latter. What attracted him to the Gurkhas was, he says, 'their sense of fun', and he agrees that many Gurkhas are 'racially mixed between Mongolians and, yes, Rajput Indians'. Describing the relationship between British royalty and the Gurkhas, he says that the latter have 'royalty of their own but admire ours'. Finally, he sums up the Gurkha character as 'family, class, clan, earthy humour, Buddhist, Hindu, fatalist' and certainly blood-thirsty, but only 'when their temper is up', remarking that they last decapitated the enemy in the service of the British Crown 'in Borneo', and adding that severing heads in armed combat is 'not significant' to them and is 'not a ritual'.

I go on to talk to some ethnic Gurkha officers, who tell me that they are not concerned about racist matters and that they certainly don't find the British unduly racist. They think that one can trust all races to be, to some extent, inevitably racist, including their own, and one officer explains how in Nepal they distinguish between 'wheat-coloured Nepalese, brown Nepalese and black Nepalese, regarding the latter as inferior people of Indian blood'. He roars with laughter and shrugs his shoulders. The British, he believes, are the least racist of people. As for the Chinese, he says that the Nepalese cannot stand them, and they are not too fond of the Indians and Muslims either, chiefly because they are corrupt, in his opinion, and he blames India for Nepal's style of government, inherited from India, and says that it is currently playing into the hands of communism and the mainland Chinese.

He also observes that: 'It's very sad that so many of yesterday's Gurkha recruits from the hills are today's communist rebels. They come from very poor communities and are, traditionally, the young men who could always find a place in the British Army as outstanding Gurkha soldiers. But, now that there is not the same demand for them, they are being persuaded by the communists to become rebels. With the British Army rejecting many more Gurkha soldiers than it accepts these days, the entrance examinations and standards are higher than before, which means that many of the ill-educated young men who used to get into the Gurkhas can no longer do so. It also means that many of those who are educated enough to get into the regiment are beginning to come from the softer towns and cities in the lowlands, and not as usual from the hard hillside and mountain communities. People in the hills, who don't want to be bullied by the Maoists and coerced into joining their rebel gangs, are leaving the hills for the lowlands.'

Major Austin tells me how he sees the character of the Gurkha soldier: 'Their temperament is generally mild-mannered, but this belies their competitive spirit. They like to win, but politely, and not in an over-the-top way. They are highly professional and very determined and modest. Their humour is not altogether like ours. They laugh a lot, but their humour is more slapstick, and they like to see the world in an amusing and sometimes childish way. But they do not understand sarcasm or satire, which does not amuse them. They also like to see you earn their respect and loyalty and not take it for granted, but you can earn it, you can win them over, which you cannot do with British Paras unless you prove that you are better than they are. And you must give Gurkha soldiers their orders in a very specific and clear way, spelling out what you want precisely and to the letter. They are very good at leading by example, so if you've done the business and proved yourself, they really respect and respond to you, but not otherwise. You must never mess them around for no reason – they do not appreciate that at all – and you must always take care to respect their requirements. There is an unwritten rule – as I indicated previously – that they will only look after you if you look after them.

'The Gurkhas believe in ghosts. Virtually every soldier has a ghost story, one of which is about a beautiful woman visiting them in their beds at night in order to sap their energy so that they cannot find the strength to fight, and they also have witch doctors in their regiments to exorcise any soldiers who become possessed. Many Gurkhas are Buddhists, but most are Hindus. They believe in one master God and many secondary gods, and they have their own pandits to counsel them. During combat they still behead people, given half a chance, so despite their jolly demeanour, they will ruthlessly have a man's head off if that's what it takes to kill the enemy. They think nothing of it. Because they are brought up in families and communities where death is a daily fact of life, and much more overt, it doesn't bother them unduly. But they are not allowed to decapitate goats with the British Army in the UK – you have to be a Muslim in Bradford to be able to do that! The goat's blood is used to bless their weapons.'

Colonel Dawson says that the Gurkhas are very respectful because: 'They come from homes in which the parents still rule the roost, so there is an in-built respect for age and seniority, which is why the Gurkhas understand better the concept of seniority. The Gurkhas obey you because they respect you, not otherwise, so you never shout and scream at them, because they would find that very funny and possibly get angry. They don't do shouting and screaming. It's not that they are afraid of hierarchy, but that they understand how to respect it, and that they are disciplined in their homes from a very young age, unlike today's Europeans. They also have respect for education and those who have proved themselves, whom they perceive to be "better" and worthy of respect, either because they are educated, or because they have medals and have been shot at.

'Gurkhas are neither obsequious nor bolshie and they are certainly not afraid to tell officers what they think. A Gurkha corporal in Borneo once told me, "no, sahib, it's far too dangerous." That was his honest view. He was not being insubordinate, he was being honest – honestly wrong, as it happens, but wrong with dignity and purpose. Many Gurkhas *do* believe in ghosts and they will put their foot down about this as well. On one occasion, a British commanding officer found a perfect jungle camp-site, with perfect water, perfect level ground and so on, but a "witch-doctor" lance corporal stepped forward and told him, "there are bad spirits here," to which the officer said, "bollocks." When the Gurkha persisted, the officer said, "bugger it, okay then," and so agreed, against his better judgement, to look for another site, moving off into the jungle, whereupon several mortar bombs fell on the site they had vacated! It's hard not to believe in spirits when that happens, or to challenge the beliefs of your men. It's hard not to allow Gurkha witch doctors in the regiment.'

Major Austin explains that the Gurkhas are very good with children. This thing about Gurkhas and children is interesting. The local junior school in Fleet, where, as has already been observed there is a Nepalese garden, loved them, and when the Gurkhas marched into Dili, the capital of East Timor, in 1999, after defeating the rebels there, they handed out sweets and balloons to local children, taking some of them by the hand and talking kindly to them.

There is an interesting link between the Gurkhas' humour and the need to be specific and spell out instructions to them in a simplified way. When Subedar Rakamsing briefed his men about going into battle with the Japanese during the Second World War (having previously heard from his white British officers what was required), he made sure that nothing got lost in translation. He told his men: 'It is to be like boxing but without following the British Queensberry rules. You jab, jab and jab again to his nose, keeping his attention high. Then you poke him in the eyes with your fingers so he cannot see. And then suddenly you kick him in the balls… our job is to kick the Japanese in the balls as hard as we can.' The *Bugle & Kukri*, which has recorded this story, observes: 'It is reported that our soldiers could not stop laughing at Rakamsing's hilarious analogy. Every time the men of C Company saw Rakamsing thereafter, they stood to attention and saluted him with the right hand and covered the testicle area with their left hands. This went on every day until the Irrawaddy was crossed and the operation started in earnest.'

Mark Austin tells me that, in his view, the American military could learn from the British, not just from Britain's military successes in jungle warfare in Malaysia, Burma and other parts of the world, and from successes in the mountains of Oman, but from its ability to win over Asian soldiers and communities when fighting in their part of the globe. In Vietnam, he thinks the Americans could have done much better, not simply by fighting more effectively, hand-to-hand in the jungle, but by winning Vietnamese hearts and minds in the process, which they did not trouble themselves to do, so their psychology was all wrong.

There can be no doubt that the British have had the knack of charming Asians and winning them over for a long time now, by showing them respect and leading by example. The British originally won the Gurkhas over in this way, almost two centuries ago, as well as winning over their more recent enemy, the Japanese (it was the English football team that most Japanese supported at the 2001 World Cup, not the American).

Colonel Dawson says that 'the Americans seem to believe that once you've got the enemy by the balls their hearts and minds will follow. Gurkhas and Brits don't behave like that. The Americans also do not seem to realise that the indiscriminate use of firepower and widespread and badly targeted bombing also destroys hearts and minds.'

The white Gurkha officers and their wives show all the signs of being from Britain's country set, quietly tucked away somewhere in country villages and towns. Hand on heart, I can say that there doesn't appear to be a townie among them. I am not talking about the not infrequently despised hunting, shooting and fishing set. Nor am I talking about the snobby and remote aristocratic set, or the inland bumpkins who do not care for foreign climes or sophisticated cities (on the contrary, many white Gurkha officers are very well travelled and reasonably internationalist in that sense). No, I suppose that I'm talking about people who prefer to live in country houses and who much prefer the outdoor life, not being overly concerned about art galleries, museums, theatres and urban pursuits. I am thinking of the July 1999 photograph of Brigadier Peter Pearson in the *Bugle & Kukri*, practising grenade throwing before leaving for Kosovo, at a barbecue party for younger Gurkha officers in Guy Stanford's splendid country house. I'm talking about clean-living simplicity and earthy matters, country walks and communing with nature, the purity of Jane Austen's *Mansfield Park* rather than the emblematic decay of Charles Dickens's *Bleak House*.

But wherever Gurkha officers and their families live, they are, like all other officer classes, destined to be a race apart, because they are, after all, much more than where they live (which is wherever they are needed when the trumpet calls). And, because they have travelled and served abroad so much, they are much more adventurous and internationally minded than most country folk who stay at home in the English countryside.

Commenting on his role as Colonel-in-Chief of the Royal Gurkha Rifles in the UK, Prince Charles has faxed me as follows: 'I have had the privilege over the past 24 years of meeting and spending time with many of the citizens of Nepal selected to serve in the British Army. Indeed, my association with Nepal and the Gurkhas has been a long and close one. I therefore know well the unerring loyalty, the infectious humour, the boundless hospitality, the astounding endurance and, above all, the remarkable bravery that constitutes the Gurkha soldier. The history of the Royal Gurkha Rifles is a tale of courage and sacrifice. It reflects a unique and enduring relationship between two peoples over nearly two centuries.

In recent times, the various roles of the Regiment have seen it engaged in the vanguard of almost all the operations and conflicts to which the United Kingdom has committed forces. The modern Gurkha soldier has proved himself where it matters most and is, deservedly, held in the very highest regard by our proud and grateful nation. The young British officer is, clearly, very fortunate to have been selected to serve alongside and lead such world-renowned fighting men. It is a challenge that can only be met with humility and selflessness.'

And of Brigadier Peter Pearson's third volume of the regimental history of the 10th Princess Mary's Own Gurkha Rifles, Prince Charles says: 'The history brings to a close the tale of this Regiment. It is a story of many tours of duty on the Hong Kong border, of service in the UK and Belize, and always of incessant training, interspersed with much sport and enjoyment. With the very future of the Brigade of Gurkhas apparently always under discussion, it is to the lasting credit of all those who served in the Regiment that so much was achieved. I am delighted to relate that the standards, traditions and spirit have all been successfully carried forward into the Royal Gurkha Rifles.'

Commenting on the 'inner faith' of the regiment that has 'been transmitted from generation to generation' (referred to by Major General Ronnie McAllister in volume two of the history), the Prince says: 'It is, of course, during operations that the true essence of a regiment is most evident. That the Gurkha Rifles managed to maintain that tradition and inner faith is remarkable. But maintain it the regiment did. Keeping pace with the changing world order and the shifts in much of the military doctrine that followed, the battalion was never found wanting... [it] built a fine reputation throughout the army for its military acumen as well as its shooting and sporting abilities.'

This inner faith to which Prince Charles refers is not unlike an inner tube – that separate inflatable tube inside the cover of our outer tyre – that keeps us going throughout life's bumpy ride. It is a tube that must never be punctured or, if it is, it must be quickly repaired and inflated once more. It is that healing and trusty inner reliance that we all need in order to keep going and be cushioned on life's long and arduous journey, that inner glow without which we do not glow at all, that binding and inescapable faith that we must keep with ourselves if we are not to lose our way and end up utterly lost. This inner faith is so important to those, such as the Gurkha tribes and many of the Nepalese, who all too frequently must look heartbreaking loss, human suffering and deprivation in the face without losing themselves and losing heart in the process.

When considering the harsh and unenviable plight of the Gurkhas and their fellow countrymen over many centuries, it takes a lot of understanding and empathy to grasp the full import of their counter-balancing inner faith and where, in their crushing circumstances, it could possibly come from. Yet come it does from this extraordinary race of sturdy little warrior people, with their big hearts and dreadfully small wallets, who look unimaginable adversity, danger and revulsion in the face, as they dig deep into the piggy bank of their inner resources.

No wonder no less a person than Prince Charles – Britain's heir apparent – considers himself 'privileged' to meet and to serve their soldiers as their Colonel-in-Chief. These are no ordinary people or soldiers. They are manly in the extreme. Of course, there is much more to life than manly pursuits, but it seems churlish to spit on them as if they were of no consequence in this dangerous and all too often cowardly world in which we all find ourselves in need of protection from time to time. Of course, as Winston Churchill once remarked, 'a medal glitters but it also casts a shadow,' and the shadow that it casts may be the shadow of death, or a shadow over civilisation itself, unless of course the medal (or gallantry award) pays tribute to those whose manliness and inner faith enables them to rise to the darkest occasions and preserve the bright light of civilisation for the rest of us.

The food at today's reunion is predictably delicious. A British Gurkha officer tells me that the regiment offers its soldiers a choice between European and Indian food, but that all of the white officers and their families have requested the latter today because they like it so much.

I have seated myself at the ethnic Gurkha – not the white British – officers' table, where I am enjoying the tenderest curried lamb cubes (chicken is also available) with plain basmati and pilau rice, dhal (lentils), tomato bhatar (grilled-tomato chutney with coriander, garlic, onions, vinegar and chilli), fresh onions and chillies, fresh mango and prawn chutneys. The poppadoms are freshly made and the delicate white wine is cool and dry.

Yes, I like their style. They get my vote any day of the week. As to their Gurkha legend, who knows?

The thing is about legends, they can only be inspired by great acts and/or people. So legends compliment and pay tribute to the people and events that figure in them, even when they are obviously exaggerated or even untrue. To be credible, legends do not have to be entirely factual – ninety per cent reality will do quite well. Not that the Gurkha legend isn't based chiefly on fact. It is. And what amazing and out-of-this world facts they are, reminding us that truth can indeed be stranger than fiction.

But these legends really do have to be entirely worthy (even when they are only fifty per cent factual!), and there are plenty of people in Britain today who seriously believe that the Gurkhas have generally fought for a worthy cause throughout their long and distinguished history, with the notable and obvious exception when they were ordered by General Dyer to fire on peaceful protestors at the Amritsar Massacre in 1919.

Dyer was obliged to resign his commission, and this, like so much else, has long disappeared into the mists of time. Today's British and ethnic Gurkha officers are a different breed entirely, as are their political paymasters. What we remember the Gurkhas for is what we know of them in recent times, and for the people they are today, which is why many people in Britain have such a great affection for them, including Prince Charles whose absence at today's reunion does not mean that he is not here in spirit, as those present see fit to think.

Today's Royal Gurkha Rifles has historical roots that go

back to the late nineteenth century – 1866 – when the 10th Princess Mary's Own Gurkha Rifles was originally formed. This remained in existence until 1994, when it decided to update itself by becoming the Royal Gurkha Rifles, with Prince Charles as its Colonel-in-Chief.

But Prince Charles is not only Colonel-in-Chief of the regiment, but also Patron of the Gurkha Welfare Fund, and the Gurkha Welfare Trust is a member of this fund. The Prince says: 'The Gurkha Welfare Trust has been established to provide a monthly welfare pension for many of the Gurkhas who fought for our freedom sixty years ago and now desperately need our help. Working through twenty-four welfare centres in Nepal, the Trust provides basic welfare pensions and medical care for over 11,500 needy Gurkha veterans and widows. The Trust was formed in 1969 with the purpose of alleviating hardship and distress among Gurkha ex-servicemen of the Crown and their dependants in Nepal, a country where there is no state welfare system and natural disasters are a common occurrence. The majority currently being helped by the Trust are Gurkha veterans of the Second World War or their widows who are now too old and frail to provide for themselves.'

When Prince Charles was visiting a Gurkha regiment in Nepal in 1980, meeting dozens of distinguished ex-soldiers who had come from far and wide to meet him, we are told by Gurkha officer Birdie Smith, in his book *Johnny Gurkha*, that 'there was a man, dressed almost biblically, standing in the queue to meet the Prince, who duly put out his hand, but the man did not respond. He was asked more than once what his old regiment was, but initially he refused to answer. Then, scowling as he spoke, he said he belonged to no regiment because he had never been enlisted. The Prince, through an interpreter, then asked him why he was in the military camp. "Come to meet you," was the abrupt answer. After further questioning it transpired that the man had walked four days to see the Prince – "We all knew you were coming" – and until that day he had never seen people shaking hands. An observer reported that the Prince of Wales was more impressed by that incident than most others that occurred during his visit to Nepal.'

I am so pleased that Major Mark Austin has wangled an invitation for me to attend today's reunion, for the simple reason that it has enabled me to get so much from the horse's mouth. It has allowed me to get so many authentic and different Gurkha voices and faces – brown and white – into the telling of this story. Thanks to the knowledgeable, no-nonsense people here today – the men (and women) behind the Gurkha image – the story of the Gurkhas has been brought up to date on matters of recruitment and education, how best to get into the regiment, the situation in Nepal, Gurkha mystique and character, cultural and racial difference, personal experience, comparisons with other glamorous regiments, and the cherished relationship with Prince Charles, all of which have been discussed with people who really know what they are talking about.

As I put this chapter to bed, here's to you, Gurkha officers and other ranks. Thank you for helping me to get at the men behind the image.

# eight

# THE HONOUR OF
# THE KUKRI

The revered *kukri* is to Nepal and the Gurkhas what the Sword of Honour is to Britain and such military institutions as Sandhurst (where the Sword of Honour is awarded to top graduates). It is a symbol of great respect and high public regard for those fighting men who have passed with battlefield honours and special distinction in the military service of their regiments and country. For this reason the *kukri* has been adopted as the national weapon of honour and glory in Nepal, where the officer class are distinguished in rank by differently graded *kukris*, and where a *kukri* is used to symbolise the King's presence.

In Evelyn Waugh's novel *Officers and Gentlemen*, the second part of his *Sword of Honour* trilogy, it is suggested that 'there should be a drug for soldiers ... to put them to sleep until they are needed. They should repose among the briar like the knights of the Sleeping Beauty; they should be laid away in their boxes in the nursery cupboard.' And this is precisely what is done with the regimental *kukri* when it is not needed, when it is put away in its scabbard and used purely for ceremonial or symbolic reasons.

I put it to Colonel Dawson, the Brigade Secretary of the Royal Gurkha Rifles in Britain, that the *kukri* is much more than a weapon of war and that it seems to symbolise the respect felt for those who have fought for the honour of their regiments in the service of the British Crown. For a soldier to have a *kukri*, or to wear it in the form of an emblem, he must achieve more than other soldiers by getting into and distinguishing himself in the Gurkhas. He must be deserving of that honour and prove himself worthy of his *kukri*, from which, in Nepal, he must never be parted, and he is under a moral obligation to use his *kukri* bravely in times of war.

But the colonel's response to this is not enthusiastic: 'Overstated, I feel.'

The *kukri* is, in many respects, the Gurkha soldier's honours degree. Whether or not, in all honesty, he seriously believes in the *kukri* as such an honourable emblem or distinction is not the point, because that is what, through its legendary history, it has become – that is what, by tradition, it represents. It is the stuff of legend and popular mythology, as well as a military distinction, and the spell that it casts is psychological. It is bigger than the man on whom the distinction is conferred, representing much more than an all-purpose tool and military weapon.

This is how many interpret the extracurricular significance of the *kukri*: as an icon of military culture, both in the national psyche of Nepal and in the regiments that have lived by it as surely as others have lived by the sword. But how does Colonel Dawson interpret the *kukri*? He tells me: 'The *kukri* is a tool and is used as such. It has no particular significance other than as a working tool. In Nepal it may have come to be regarded as an icon, but much of the above overstates the case.'

So much is said about this world-famous and oddly curved little fighting knife, which has become the symbol, not only of Nepal but also of the Royal Gurkha Rifles in the UK, with its two battalions, one in the UK and one in Brunei. It is as symbolic to Gurkha men of war, and the Nepalese nation and its various tribes today, as are the spear to the Zulu and the sword to the Samurai. It would seem to stand for an idealised concept of bravery and method of fighting, for heroism and honour in gruesome hand-to-hand fighting by men of determination and faith – faith in themselves to be able to defend themselves, faith in the rightness of their cause, and above all faith in the outstanding martial history and purpose of their race.

The *kukri* also seems to stand for an idealised past. To the nostalgic minds of those who prefer the *kukri* to the machine-age tank, it is a more honourable weapon, cleaner, nobler, braver and more dignified than the tank, because one must have the guts to engage one's opponent, eyeball to eyeball, in fair and equal combat. (Truth to tell, soldiers who take this view may also believe that the *kukri* is more fun than the tank.)

When we talk of military honour we talk of good personal character, of loyalty and honesty, of honourable and uncowardly conduct on and off the field of battle, of upholding the honour of the regiment, and of respect for all that is perceived to be honourable. But if these values are not to be false – if this talk is to be anything more than hollow – they have to be backed up with action. In the case of the Gurkhas, *kukri* action.

Because it is a romanticised symbol of honour that has captured the imagination of the entire world, this glittering and much-revered little weapon is nowadays used as much for ceremonial purposes as it is for hand-to-hand fighting. And, in the country in which it originates, its most common use is for neither of these purposes, but for everyday tasks such as cutting and butchering meat, skinning animals, peeling vegetables, and hacking, shaping and chopping wood. It is used for these tasks by both the valley dwellers and the hill peoples of Nepal, many of whom still carry it around with them in their belts or sashes, and by all accounts it has been in use there since the seventeenth century.

In short, the *kukri* is an all-purpose tool and the purposes to which it is put are as peaceful as they are warlike, as domestic and civilian as they are military. The *kukri* is at the very heart of the tradition and culture of Nepal, and, as a very good friend or a deadly foe, it mirrors the duality of human nature and the nature of mankind.

But to return to the *kukri*'s more elevated uses, we can see that its historic renown as an instrument of war is matched only by its significance in ceremony and ritual. In royal ceremonies the *kukri* is predictably splendid and can inspire even spiritual and mystical qualities. It is for this reason that, when the King of Nepal is unable to attend any ceremony or festival in his palace, his own golden *kukri* is placed on his throne, so that he can be there in spirit. Reverence and obeisance are paid to him through his *kukri*, such is its intended spiritual power.

On these enchanting royal occasions, when the King's *kukri* is placed on his throne by his ministers or members of his family, the knife is transformed from a weapon of war into an emblem of peace and enchantment. In this role it reflects veneration, awe and deep respect for the crown, culture, customs and traditions on behalf of which it has been used so savagely in so many wars throughout the centuries. But in battle it has wielded a lurid and lethal enchantment: against Turks, Germans, Italians and Japanese, Persians, Arabs and North Africans, Koreans, Malaysians and Indonesians, to mention but a few.

And from all these bloodbaths it has proudly emerged, gleaming once again, cleansed of all its enemies' blood, to survive as an eternal symbol of the determination, honour and manliness of the Gurkha soldiers and the Nepalese nation. The earliest known *kukri*, owned by Gorkha king, Rajadrada Shah in 1627, can be seen today in the National Museum in Kathmandu (also on display there is another eighteenth-century heavy-duty *kukri*, dating back to 1749, which was the property of Kanji Kale Paned and is much heavier than today's *kukris*).

It is said that the *kukri* came into its own against the long spears, two-edged long swords, wrist-guard short swords and daggers of Prithvi Narayan Shah's opponents. These weapons were no match for the versatility of the *kukri*, and could not parry this curved little knife satisfactorily, if at all. Because of its efficiency in hand-to-hand warfare, the *kukri* quickly became the preferred and fabled weapon of Nepal. The shape and structure of Rajadrada Shah's *kukri* has hardly changed at all since 1627 and I am tempted to suppose that its peculiar curved blade is shaped to follow the line of an opponent's neck! I have absolutely no proof or evidence of this, but why else would it be curved?

*Kukri* blades are made of steel and the best-quality examples today are those of European steel, whereas *kukris* made in Nepal are of poorer steel. Handles are usually made of wood or buffalo horn. Today's *kukris* remain broad-bladed, just as they were in the seventeenth century, with the same grooved cutting edge, and the same handles and notch at the base of the blade. The handle of Rajadrada Shah's *kukri* is of carved wood, as would have befitted a Gorkha king in those days, while these days they are ivory, heavy metal and other handles. I am told that the grooved cutting edge is designed to cleverly deflect and so reduce the impact of a blow from an enemy's sabre, sword or dagger by tilting and turning it aside instead of meeting it head on. The *kukri* user briefly lets the diminished force of the blow vibrate all the way down the blade to the notch at its base, then gives a quick twist of the notch to unbalance the offending sabre, sword or dagger and disarm the enemy.

The Gurkha Museum in Winchester describes the action of the *kukri* thus: 'A nick in the blade close to the handle serves the purpose of preventing blood from reaching the handle and is also symbolic of the Hindu Trinity of Bramah, Vishnu and Shiva. Two small knives are fitted at the top of the scabbard, one blunt (Chakmak) and the other sharp (Karda). The correct use of the former is for starting a fire with a flint stone and as a sharpening stone, and the latter is a skinning or general purpose knife... The wrist action with which the *kukri* is wielded makes it extremely effective in the hands of one accustomed to using it... there is also a sacrificial *kukri* with a longer blade and handle suitable for gripping with two hands... little used except for sacrificing animals at festival time. The popular myth that blood must be shed every time a *kukri* is drawn from its scabbard is untrue and probably stems from the fact that if drawn in anger, then it was unlikely to be replaced without being used! Similar stories of the *kukri* being used as a throwing knife can be disbelieved.'

In the Nepalese Army, high-ranking officers are distinguished by the exquisitely tasteful patterns etched into the blades of their *kukris*. Senior members of Nepal's royal family have similar but even more splendid etchings on their *kukris*. Army officers' *kukris* have semicircular insignias, while those of royalty bear circular insignias designating high caste. The idea of royalty and army wedded together, the latter in the loyal and devoted service of the former, is symbolised by these priceless and decorative *kukris*, some of the handles of which are inlaid with emeralds and other precious stones.

The scabbards for these very superior *kukris* feature gold and silver mountings, whereas most standard scabbards are made of wood, leather or bone and incorporate very useful tiny pockets – not unlike miniature bullet pouches – into which tweezers, pen knives, nail clippers or scissors and the like can be inserted. The more decorative standard scabbards are inlaid with brass, coloured glass, turquoise or lapis lazuli, and some of the ivory *kukri* handles imitate animals' heads. But, whatever materials are used for the scabbards and handles, and whatever designs are employed to beautify these, there is no getting away from the fact that the *kukri* remains a lethal fighting knife. Similarly, however mystical it may become in the ceremonies of Nepal and the Gurkha regiments wherever they may be serving in the world, there is of course nothing in the least mystical or ceremonial about the use to which the *kukri* is put in military combat. One must remember this famed efficiency when releasing a sharp *kukri* from its scabbard. The back, or blunt, edge of the knife is held towards the body, so that the cutting edge is facing away from it.

So much for the military, ceremonial and domestic uses of the *kukri*. But it is also used for religious purposes, demonstrating yet again its spiritual significance in the overall scheme of things in Gurkha and Nepali minds.

The *kukri* is used for severing the heads of buffalo, sheep and goats at religious festivals, where it is thought that the higher the blood spurts into the air, the greater the blessings that rain down on the people. It is also used to spill animal blood and God's blessings on weapons of war, and here again we are reminded of its dual role as a spiritual symbol and a military tool.

The emblem on the badge of the Royal Gurkha Rifles in Britain shows two upturned *kukris* meeting at the top, their naked blades crossing, as if to convey a pledge from those whose profession it is to use the *kukri* when fighting for the honour of the regiment and in the service of the British Crown: 'Cross my heart and hope to die!' (or, to quote the actual regimental motto, 'Better to die than to be a coward').

# nine

# THE GURKHAS
# ON EVEREST

It is 1953 and we are witnessing the first conquest of the highest mountain in the world. Attached to the expedition are a group of Gurkha soldiers, doing what they do so well, which is 'trying their hand at more exciting work', according to the leader of the expedition, John Hunt.

These Gurkhas are led by a 32-year-old British Gurkha officer called Charles Wylie (now in retirement in Hampshire, but referred to earlier in this book), who is a mountain climber with considerable experience. He has been invited to join this world-famous expedition by John Hunt, who has written of Wylie in his book *The Ascent of Everest*.

Having spent most of the war in a Japanese prison camp, Wylie has emerged with a remarkable selflessness and sympathy for others, and an extraordinary faith and cheerful disposition that is perhaps hard to credit after his ordeal at

the hands of the merciless Japanese. All the expedition
equipment has been carefully prepared and documented by
Wylie, and since he has good Alpine and UK experience of
climbing, he is at home with the likes of Hunt, another
accomplished mountaineer and army officer (Royal
Engineers). Helping to lead the ascent are Edmund Hillary,
a mountaineering beekeeper from New Zealand (who will
be knighted for his achievement, whilst Hunt will become a
life peer), and Tenzing Norgay, known as Sherpa Tenzing, a
renowned Nepalese mountaineer.

This was all a very long time ago, more than half a century in
fact, but to those of us who were around at the time – I was in
my fourteenth year – it seems like only yesterday. It was three
years ahead of the short-lived Anglo-French invasion of the
Suez Canal in 1956, and two years ahead of the first publication
of the allegorical novel, *Lord of the Flies* in 1955, by William
Golding. Four years after the assent of Everest, the angry young
man, John Osborne, wrote his landmark play, *Look Back in
Anger*. The Gurkhas were helping Everesters to climb Mount
Everest towards the end of an era that was coming swiftly to a
close, when others had other things on their minds.

Certainly, the memory of Everest remains vivid in Colonel
Wylie's mind to this day. He explains that he was in charge of
five Gurkha NCOs, who had been given leave of absence to
report to him during the expedition. The NCOs' task was to
supervise the porters and guard the expedition and its supplies,
in particular the heavy treasure chests, full of coins with which
to pay the porters and others, and to make the necessary
purchases along the way. To make sure that no thieving hands

could find their way into these chests, they spread blankets over them, sleeping on top of them at night, rifles to hand.

It was also left to Charles Wylie to engage a small army of so-called 'coolies' to carry the baggage on what turned out to be a seventeen-day journey. He had to muster some three hundred and fifty local men, each of whom were recorded in a pay book, so that they could receive their wages and an advance of pay. The Brigade of Gurkhas had permitted the voluntary services of five of its NCOs to assist Charles Wylie in his task and, when the coolies joined the expedition at Kathmandu to accompany the caravan, they refused to accept the flimsy paper currency that was offered them, stating a preference to be paid in hard cash instead. So the expedition was obliged to take half its treasure in Nepali coins. Quite a heavy weight to haul up mountains!

Because the Sherpa tongue was a mystery to the mountain climbers, the expedition had to rely on Charles Wylie's Gurkhali, because most Sherpas had some knowledge of this, in addition to their own tongue, and could at least converse with him and his Gurkha soldiers. In addition to his mountaineering duties, Wylie was in charge of co-ordinating all equipment, supplies, labour and transport, whilst also fulfilling a secretarial role. By the time the expedition got going, Hunt noted that Charles and Tenzing Norgay had 'done a magnificent job' in getting the expedition off to an 'encouraging well-organized start'.

But there was a memorable social occasion before they left, when the climbers were entertained by the King of Nepal, no less, as well as the Indian Ambassador, at a reception that was organized at the British Embassy in their honour.

Mount Everest took its name, in 1849, from Sir George Everest, former Surveyor-General of India. The first man to think seriously about climbing it was the legendary Gurkha officer, Charles Bruce, who had travelled extensively in the Himalayas and had long been an enthusiastic mountain climber. It was the wild and colourful Bruce who had personally wrestled and boozed with his Gurkha soldiers, and had a reputation for womanising with their wives too, when he was not organising cross-country races for Gurkha soldiers, up and down mountain and valley slopes. Affectionately known to his native Gurkhas as 'the bear', he was one of those hands-on officers who did not know how to be standoffish with his men. But he was not every officer's cup of tea. Some of the officer class regarded him as too much of a 'character' and an exhibitionist for their liking. He was unashamedly of the bulldog breed and, if anyone was likely to have been the first to think of climbing Everest, it was certainly Bruce, who was by far the most obvious candidate at the time.

But, when Lord Curzon came up with the first sponsorship plan for climbing Everest, the British government ruled it out, reportedly on the grounds that it might upset the Russians! If anything was calculated to make the likes of Bruce climb the mountain, it was of course the delightful prospect of upsetting the Russians.

The first climber to get anywhere near Everest was another army officer, John Noel, who entered Tibet in 1913. He did so, off record and suitably disguised, and then proceeded to get within forty miles of the forbidding and politically forbidden mountain. Eventually, an Everest Committee was set up, the first president of which was Younghusband of Tibet.

Not until 1921 was there a proper reconnaissance of the world's highest mountain, which the British in particular so much wanted to climb (that they did it first seems only fitting in view of their obsession with it). Virtually every adventurer and mountaineer of the Victorian Empire was drawn to Everest. They proudly called themselves Everesters and they were, without exception, romantic upper-middle-class types, whose spirit of bravado was such that they wanted to conquer whatever it was that seemed unconquerable. George Leigh Mallory – that 'magical spirit of youth' who died on Everest in 1924 – said that he wanted to climb this magical and irresistible mountain 'because it's there'.

Nobody seriously asked *why* it should be climbed, or what use it would be, or if they did the Everesters were not listening. Everyone seemed to agree with Mallory that the mountain had to be climbed, simply because it was there, and that's what one does with mountains. One instinctively climbs them, some of us more successfully than others. University professors and graduates, army officers and generals, public schoolboys and gentlemen adventurers, and some members of parliament and diplomats, all wanted to climb Everest. The mountain had gone to their heads. They had time, money and leisure on their hands, so the world was their oyster. And of all the places they could think of going, it was to the top of Everest. They wanted greatness by performing great acts, by courageously testing themselves to the limit and being at one with nature. They wanted a clean and healthy life and they were all head over heels in favour of Everest.

Either their lives were otherwise empty – so they

desperately needed a mountain to fulfil themselves – or they were so full of themselves that they would stop at nothing, not a mountain, not the world, not the ends of the earth. Perhaps they were driven to be at one with nature because they found it impossible to be at one with human kind?

Perhaps, if yesterday's men were generally much more rugged and physical than most men are these days, they were attracted to mountain climbing as a test of their physical endurance. The Everester generation was unashamedly into manly pursuits and seriously intent on breeding a race of boys and men who really were expected to go out into the world and prove themselves, fairly and squarely, as men (mummy's boys were definitely out of favour). So there was no doubting their courage, or indeed their extraordinary spirit of adventure.

Of course it is possible that these early mountain climbers were simply romantics. Romance was alive and well still in nineteenth and early twentieth century Britain, which had inherited the tradition from medieval times, when English literature recounted the marvellous adventures of the chivalric hero. In nineteenth-century literature, romance featured scenes and incidents far removed from common life that were surrounded by mystery and in an atmosphere of strangeness and adventure, and all of this and more was to be had in the climbing of Mount Everest and/or the building of an empire on distant Oriental shores. So it is quite possible that mountain climbing was a romantic escape from common life and its dreadfully commonplace people. In which case, it stands to reason that romantic individualists of the bulldog breed would have romanticised a mountain such as Everest.

If Wordsworthian and other poets could write about such beauteous landscapes, why wouldn't others want to go out there and walk or climb them? And if the earth's geological history could throw up mountains whenever two continents collided for the purpose – compressing the sediment between them into mountain chains – then the Victorian and post-Victorian British were showing that they could throw up mountain climbers in the different continents of their empire and elsewhere, who were breaking upon the scene almost like an event of nature themselves! Just as there had long been orogenies occurring in the history of mountain formations, suddenly there were periods of mountain climbing occurring in the wake of these mountains, in which men were determined to conquer their formations. To many, it all seemed part of an inevitable life cycle – man must explore and eventually tame nature. Just as he must tame wild animals, he must tame wild landscapes as well. As for mountains, if he couldn't tame them exactly, he could at least experience them.

Mountaineering began in the eighteenth century when, in 1786, Mont Blanc was climbed in Europe by the Frenchmen, Michel Paccard and Jacques Balmat. In 1857 the English Alpine Club was founded, soon to be followed by the foundation of Continental European clubs (occasional members of the English clubs were so nutty, evidently, that they reportedly ran naked through Swiss hotels to demonstrate their individuality!) The sport of mountaineering developed in the nineteenth century when the Matterhorn was climbed in 1865 by Edward Whymper's expedition. But the sport was not confined to Europe. In Africa, Hans Meyer and Ludwig Purtscheller climbed Mount Kilimanjaro in 1889, and Sir Halford Mackinder climbed Mount Kenya during the same year.

But, if British and European mountain climbers were simply hopeless romantics, it was all to the good as far as Everest and those who subsequently made a living from it were concerned, because the romance was becoming a global sport, and the mountain that everyone wanted to climb was, of course, that splendid jewel Mount Everest, the highest and most romanticised mountain in the world. But, whatever they were, these early mountaineers, however they were driven and motivated – romantically or otherwise – they would explore and discover whatever there was to explore and discover. There was, it seemed, no stopping them.

The romance of mountains was new to the ethnic Gurkha soldiers who followed their white officers into the Himalayas. A great many of these Gurkhas had long been animists, who felt at one with nature and believed that the physical world was permeated by a spirit (*anima mundi*), which is why they regarded different mountains, valleys, trees, rocks and rivers as holy, and had been known to worship them.

Everest was a dramatic and imperial mountain that perfectly suited the imperial drama of the time and that drama was being enacted in Britain more than most other countries. It was being enacted in adventurous France as well – as it had been enacted in Spain, Holland and Portugal previously – but nowhere was it being dramatised on such a grand and passionate scale as it was in Britain. The modern world was being made by the discovery, advancement and inevitable exploitation of the old world, so many parts of which remained to be explored and conquered, and this was a peculiarly Victorian process, the legacy of which came from the seventeenth century when Britain first invented, not only democracy for itself, but the navigational and maritime sciences as well.

It is against this fascinating and eccentric background of Britain's extraordinary love affair with this most extraordinary and highly symbolic mountain – beginning with Gurkha officer Charles Bruce – that Gurkha officer Charles Wylie took his Gurkha NCOs to the Himalayas in the 1950s. And, of all the soldiers (as opposed to officers) who could have been involved in such a great feat as conquering Everest for the first time, it really had to be none other than ethnic Gurkhas. Down from the hills of Nepal and perfectly at home with mountains, valleys and rocky terrain, they also loved an unconquerable challenge, and they knew as well as any Britisher how to 'play up, play up, and play the game', win or lose, albeit winning more often than not. And the game was a serious one – succeeding in getting to the top of Everest, without coming to grief in the process.

The eyes of the world were upon them and, when Edmund Hillary and Tenzing Norgay stepped onto the summit on 29 May 1953, they caught the imagination of the world. It was an historic achievement to get to the top of the highest mountain in the world, but it could not have been done by two men alone, and crucial to their success was the back-up team of Colonel Wylie and his Gurkhas. The expedition was not just a milestone for international mountaineering, but for the

Brigade of Gurkhas as well, proving, once again, that their men are a match for such challenges.

Prince Philip, the Duke of Edinburgh, said at the time that 'in human terms of physical effort and endurance alone' the first ascent of Everest 'will live in history as a shining example to all mankind'.

At the time, most people perceived the conquering of Everest in the same light as later generations perceived the landing of the first astronaut on the moon. They were awestruck. It was unbelievable and unheard of. Today, almost any old Tom, Dick or Harry can pay professionals to take them up part or perhaps all of this mythical mountain. But, in those days, Everest was generally regarded as invincible. Everyone had heard of it – including those who had no idea where it was on the world map – but few, if any, seriously believed that it would ever be climbed. Since 1953, Everest has been climbed this way and that by many different people. It has been climbed solo, while some have paraglided off it. So many people have gone to Everest to camp out on it, putting it on the map as a tourist destination. A blind man has paid professionals to take him up it. In their efforts to tackle its ridges and great faces, many have been assisted by Gurkha veterans and Sherpas of Gorkha and other origins, who have generated some income or supplemented their pensions from this demand from the outside world to scale Everest.

That a serving Gurkha officer, ably assisted by Gurkha NCOs, played such an important role in the first assent of the world's highest mountain, is yet another first for the Gurkhas.

# ten

# THERE ARE NO GURKHAS?

In some books the author's perspective is upfront from the first page, whereas in others it has to be explored and unravelled. Some writers stick to their own perspective throughout, while others embrace perspectives other than their own. Some perspectives win our sympathy and/or approval, while others do not. This all goes to show that both writing and reading are highly subjective affairs.

A perspective that is not generally given in books on the Gurkhas is that of the ethnic Gurkhas and the Nepalis themselves. This is what I want to offer in this book, as a counterbalance to the perspective of the white British officer class. But it is not easy to access either the Gurkha perspective or the wider Nepalese perspective, because Nepal does not have a strong tradition of literature such as exists in English, or a great chattering class of Gurkha soldiers (who are, in fact, often pretty tight-lipped when it comes to talking to journalists and authors).

It stands to reason that books written about Gurkha soldiers by their officers will be written from a military perspective – and in most cases from the perspective of the social class and/or race of the white officers in question. The writer has a specific, and often limited, readership in mind. (The same is true, for example, of academic books that are written from a narrow perspective.)

In *Warrior Gentlemen – 'Gurkhas' in the Western Imagination*, Professor Lionel Caplan tells us: 'The collective attachment to common cultural and social perspectives on the part of both military writers and their audiences … raises a host of questions about the nature of the Gurkha reality which this literature purports to describe … they tend to constitute the Gurkhas in the very process of writing about them… The Gurkha can thus best be understood as a fiction. This is not to imply that Gurkhas do not really exist, or that those who write about them are deliberately fabricating lies and fallacies… these writings … can be labelled fictions in the sense of something 'fashioned'… Gurkhas exist in the context of the military imagination, and are thereby products of the officers who command and write about them; outside that setting, it can be argued, there are no Gurkhas, only Nepalis.'

It is true that, in the British imagination, the Gurkhas exist, almost entirely in military literature (although they do crop up in travel literature as well). And because there are no films about them – as there are about, say, the Bedouin (David Lean's romantic and spectacular *Lawrence of Arabia* is perhaps the best example) – the Gurkhas are, for the most part, a literary construct in most people's minds. They have a literary rather than a screen image and this literary image features in the media as well as in military books about them. It is also true that one likes to hope that there is more to the Gurkhas than their fine soldierly virtues – not that one would expect to discover this 'other' reality of Johnny Gurkha in books by military authors (any more than one would expect to find an 'other' English, Welsh, Scottish or Irish soldier in books about them by military authors, or an 'other' white British officer in books of which they are the authors). Books are written and read for different purposes. Military and academic minds do not share the same concerns or enthusiasms, and, as for novelists, they will have a different set of priorities again.

For example, when E.M. Forster wrote his widely acclaimed novel *A Passage to India*, he wrote, with common consent, from the perspective of a novelist in search of the spiritual essence of India. It was very much an educated, sensitive, liberal-minded and racially respectful English account of the spiritual in India, written from the sheltered and highly privileged background of the rich Indian princes whose guest Forster was in that country. But the fact that he was writing from the purely spiritual perspective, and in rarefied circumstances, was not a limitation. He did not write a lesser novel on account of having a particular perspective. We know exactly where he is coming from (just as we know exactly where British officers are coming from when they write from their own perspective about their Gurkha soldiers, and we do not expect anything more or less from them either).

We are told by Professor Peter Mudford, formerly of the University of London, in his book *The Art of Celebration* (in fictional literature), that 'alternation of perspective' is at work in Forster's novel, and this cannot be said for most military books. But we can be in no doubt that perspectives are alive and well in all forms of literature – factual, fictional, academic and military – and that this is by no means a mark against them. So we should not be surprised by perspectives, least of all in military literature, where a single perspective is much more controlling and visible than elsewhere and certainly more limiting. A single perspective may or may not be too shallow and one-dimensional, but it is understandable in military books.

When we look at the romantic perspective of T.E. Lawrence's *Seven Pillars of Wisdom*, on which David Lean's film is based, we are reminded that film directors and authors do not need to make excuses for the perspective of their works and, while there are always other perspectives to be explored, that is not always possible or desirable within the boundary of a particular book or film. But, in the case of the Gurkhas, with their strong racial identity, one feels that an authentic Gurkha perspective is as necessary as that of the white British Gurkha officer. Professor Caplan is right to observe that, in order to raise the military author's perspective above the level of gun smoke, there is a need to include ethnic Gurkha voices, as these illuminate the social and historical setting and heighten the reader's appreciation of how the Gurkhas are, how they sound, what it is like to be a Gurkha in the opinion of a Gurkha, and how they perceive themselves and others. But, as has already been observed, this is by no means easy in the case of the Gurkhas (in fact, there are not many Gurkha voices in Caplan's book, even though he went all the way to Nepal to write it).

Even so, previous chapters in this book do contain some revealing quotes from ethnic Gurkha – as opposed to white British – officers, and for this chapter I am glad to say that I have managed to research other material from Gurkha and Nepalese sources.

Caplan refers to 'romantic approvers' of the Gurkhas who focus only on the 'positive assessments' of their Gurkha soldiers. This phenomenon is hardly surprising. One would hope that British officers do have positive rather than negative things to say about the soldierly qualities of their men, otherwise it would be a very poor army indeed (and very poorly inspired and led). And since such a high standard is set for soldiers to get into the Gurkhas, why would they not have so many positive military qualities, and why would their officers not openly approve of them so enthusiastically, since that is what they value most, and what counts most in battle?

Such considerations are doubtless lost on professors of anthropology, who write from different perspectives. Yet I am not out of sympathy with an academic approach to military texts or matters. In common with others, I believe that it has a useful part to play. But, like the military officer class itself, academics have to get their perspectives right too. Professor Caplan tells us that 'the Gurkhas are transformed into pets' in the literature that is written about them. Try telling that to the men who went to the Falklands! Pets stay at home, surely? No, what they are transformed into are guard dogs, if we want to trade metaphors. No doubt, if you select your books carefully, you can prove the Gurkha-pet argument, but it is by no means true of all books.

The thing to remember about the Gurkhas as a subject for literature is that they will not conform to new or even old notions and explanations. You have to take them as you find them, whether you are an academic, military author, historian, journalist or novelist. In view of what is known of their factual historical record, which is by and large indisputable, you will have a hard job misrepresenting them in works of literature. The fact is that they do have many 'positive' qualities – politeness, responsibility, self-discipline, loyalty, resource-fulness, humour, amazing courage, fearlessness, heroism, human warmth – and they are of course physically very fit. If this makes them 'larger than life' characters in the view of, ahem, 'smaller than life' anthropology professors, if this makes them too fantastical in books by military authors who approve of their qualities – so what? Readers are not fools. They can make up their own minds and take with a pinch of salt whatever they think needs to be taken with a pinch of salt. They can see through and around things. They are not duped by authors. And if the emphasis on Gurkha qualities is sometimes too strong, surely that is understandable, for the simple reason that they offer a better alternative or stereotype to 'the crime and violence on an unprecedented scale' and the 'thugs and psychopaths' who 'murder and maim and torture and never have a finger laid on them for it' in British society today, as referred to by the former British Army officer and novelist George MacDonald Fraser in his book entitled *Quartered Safe Out Here*.

Every author brings his own vision and the influence of his educational and cultural background to the writing of a book – just as readers bring theirs to reading it – and white Gurkha officers writing about their Gurkha soldiers are no exception. The challenge for authors is how best to strike a balance between their own and others people's perspectives. When writing a factual book about others, an author generally hesitates to allow too much of himself into the story, for the simple reason that it is supposed to be about them and not himself. However, this is not the case when most white British officers write about their Gurkha soldiers, because they are writing entirely from personal experience and with the fixed perception and voice of authority. In short, they are writing from a narrow military standpoint. We are invited to take their word for what they say, while not expecting too much of Professor Mudford's 'alternation of perspective' from them.

But if, like me, an author has no personal experience of professional soldiering, and yet has accepted the challenge of writing a book about the Gurkhas, then he is in a position to broaden the boundaries by including the voices of many others; he is in a position to provide the 'broader view' referred to by one of the white officers quoted in chapter seven of this book.

In the belief that they know best, many of the white British officers writing about the Gurkhas have been, naturally enough, jealously possessive of their subjects, and many of them have not gone out of their way to consider or include too many 'other' voices or perceptions. There are exceptions, of course, but in general most of them stick doggedly to their own, entirely predictable, perspective, as do other professionals, such as lawyers or doctors, for example, when writing about their professions.

But let's get back to how the Gurkha soldiers see themselves. An entirely different perspective is suggested by a letter purporting to come from some Gurkha discontents who had joined the Indian National Army in the days of British India. The letter was circulated by the Japanese to prisoners in their camps in Burma. If it was not a fake, it certainly shows that not all Gurkhas perceived themselves as honorary Europeans in the service of the British, and even if it was a fake, it nevertheless offered an alternative perspective to desperate Gurkha soldiers at a time when they could have saved their own skins by switching sides (and thereby changing their perspective), had they so wished.

We are told by the former Gurkha officer Birdie Smith, in *Johnny Gurkha*, that the letter read: 'Dear Gurkha soldiers! One cannot describe the condition of the Gurkhas who were sent to fight in the Far East. The British left us, the Gurkhas, to meet a living death, to face hardship and fight against odds in the jungle of Sittaung and Moulmein, when they withdrew themselves. The whole of the youth of our land have been snatched from our land. Who are to defend our sacred Nepal from the Chinese aggression from the North? The British have fully exploited us. Why fight for them who want to keep you slaves? Why not join hands with those who are to destroy and wipe them totally thus bringing happiness to all.

Your Gurkha Brothers

Indian National Army.'

Gurkha soldiers serving in the British Army were said to be contemptuous of this letter and, according to Birdie Smith, it was 'used by the prisoners for a variety of purposes! Having failed by lectures and the written word, the Japanese tried various tactics, ranging from sheer brutality to bribery by offering luxuries, and even appealing to the Gurkhas to side with them because of a distinct similarity in physical appearances... Before they were separated by too many miles, a handful of officers risked death or, at the best, severe beatings, by making secret visits to see their beloved Gurkhas who had served them so well.'

If some British officers in Gurkha regiments have 'romantically approved' of such conduct from their soldiers, who can blame them? Certainly not me.

A young Gurkha rifleman, Aitasing Gurung MC, who was also a prisoner of war, is reported by Smith to have written: 'A sick man sent to the hospital never returned recovered. Due to the scarcity of medicines in the hospitals no sick man survived during our days in prison. Sometimes the Japs would ask us to join their army and on negative answer, they would treat us more severely. They even opened fire on our camp... No one at that time hoped of being able to return safe to his homeland.'

An alternative and negative perspective on Gurkha soldiers was offered by Orde Wingate of the Royal Artillery, who was Britain's commander of the Chindits during the

Burma campaign against the Japanese. He made himself unpopular with a lot of British Gurkha and other officers who, by all accounts, thought him pushy, vain, pretentious and overrated. He got right up the noses of British Gurkha officers when he criticised their Gurkhas soldiers, and Birdie Smith has written: 'Wingate was to criticize the Gurkhas as being mentally unsuited for the role given them during the first Chindit expedition. Events since 1948 have shown the Gurkhas to be ideal troops for guerrilla and an-guerrilla warfare in the jungle. Their fitness, ability to carry great weights, and cheerful patience in discomfort and adversity have always existed. But, by splitting the men up, by mixing units and, quite simply, not understanding that Gurkha soldiers need a different type of leadership to the British, Wingate failed to exploit their basic qualities. Let that be an end of the debate. As far as the Gurkhas were concerned, the first expedition proved nothing that was not known before and achieved little, while the lessons, if any, were mainly ones showing what must not be repeated.'

So much for Wingate's perspective! We are thus reminded how tricky these perspectives are and how they need to be qualified, as far as possible, when featured in literature. Too often they tell us more about the person whose perspective it is than the persons to whom it is supposed to apply.

When it comes to a social and historical perspective on the Gurkhas, a book by the Nepalese historian Kamal Raj Singh Rathaur is perhaps enlightening. In *The British and the Brave* he say: 'it has been estimated that by the end of the Second World War... the cost to Nepal in dead alone was more than

10,000 men' and he is in no doubt of the historical facts when it comes to the subject of Gurkha bravery 'the turbulent history of these little fighters has created a myth of the Gallantry, the myth of the bravest of the brave', which, as George MacDonald Fraser would say, 'is no myth at all.'

The following quote from Field Marshal Lord Slim which appears at the beginning of Rathaur's book: 'The Almighty created in the Gurkha an ideal infantryman, indeed an ideal Rifleman, brave, tough, patient, adaptable, skilled in field-craft, intensely proud of his military record and unswerving loyalty. Add to this his honesty in word and deed, his parade perfection, and his unquenchable cheerfulness, then service with Gurkhas is for any soldier an immense satisfaction.'

If such literature about Gurkha soldiers is 'best understood as a fiction', as Professor Caplan suggests, perhaps in reality there are no Gurkhas as we know them, other than in the minds of the white British officers who write about them and present them in a certain – fictional? – way. There may be some other Gurkhas behind the mask, whom we do not know, because the Gurkhas that we do know are no more than our own reflection, and this is very far from who they actually are. All this implies that the Gurkhas are not Gurkhas, but somebody else.

Earlier in this book I was pleased to introduce Major Laxmi Bantawa of the Royal Gurkha Rifles in the UK, who is, of course, 'somebody else' in addition to being a Gurkha officer and a man of war, and I am interested to discover who that other person is. Professor Caplan has observed that too many military books about the Gurkhas do 'not include the subject of the discourse'. In other words they talk *about*

Gurkha soldiers rather than to or with them, excluding rather than including their voices. But this is not such a book. Having met and spoken at length to Laxmi on several occasions, I am only too pleased to return to him again here, and I know that he and the Royal Gurkha Rifles are more than happy that he is speaking for himself in his own words and from his own perspective. It is true that the Royal Gurkha Rifles wanted to see how he was to be quoted, in return for giving its permission for him to be interviewed by me, but the regiment approved his copy without changing a single word, which is very reassuring in view of the political as well as the personal nature of the interview that I conducted with him.

Probably one of the reasons why Professor Caplan thinks that Gurkhas have sometimes been regarded as 'pets' by some writers is because of books such as *The Call of Nepal* by John Cross, a former British Gurkha officer who settled in Nepal. Cross tells us: 'The eastern Gurkha is like a cat: friendship cannot be forced and chemistry takes some time to work. The westerners are more like dogs: it was productive to make positive advances.' This is the perspective of a white British officer, but by no means all white British or ethnic Gurkha officers share it.

Now, Laxmi Bantawa is a Rai from the eastern part of Nepal to which Cross refers. (Rais and Limbus come from the east, Magars and Gurungs from the west.) Yet when I meet Laxmi he seems readily approachable and affable enough and, as far as I can tell, the chemistry is working instantly and perfectly well between us. He is not standing on ceremony, so the chemistry doesn't seem to be taking 'some time to work', as Cross suggests. So, suspecting that these generalisations about groups of people are prone to be less than perfect, I ask Laxmi whether Cross's cat-and-dog observation holds good and whether he regards himself as a cat rather than a dog.

He replies: 'Cross Sahib's thoughts probably arise from the different ways in which the agricultural communities in each region live. In the east, homes are separated and are in the centre of an individual's land or on top of the land where they can see most of the area of the land that they own. In the west all landowners live together in villages, commuting to their land. That might be the reason why easterners are a bit quieter than the westerners at the beginning, when they meet people. It's because of the environmental influence. But, changing by the day, I see more development in the east than in the western part of Nepal. About ten years ago, the westerners were more educated than the easterners.'

So, from the perspective of an eastern Nepalese Gurkha, his brothers in the west of the country may well have been more readily approachable, even chatty, because they have been much more close and communal and therefore communicative, more used to company and ready conversation, and also better educated than their eastern counterparts, who have always been more reserved and, perhaps because they were less educated, less instantly communicative. But he is clear that nowadays all this is changing (again we are reminded that these perspectives need qualifying).

On the other hand, commenting on the difference between the Gurkha soldier's long-standing traditional image and the modern man behind that image today, Laxmi believes that some things stay the same: 'Although there have been a lot of changes in the army, the Gurkha ethos has not been changed and must not be changed. The Gurkha ethos is unique and this is why the Gurkhas are still maintaining the highest standards in the British Army. And I am very glad that they are doing an outstanding job in the twenty-first century as well. The Gurkhas are still brave enough, tough, have patience, and are adaptable, skilled in field craft and proud of their military record. They are loyal, honest, cheerful, hard-working and have the highest standards on parade. Today's Gurkhas are more educated, intelligent and have a broader vision. Hence, the Gurkha "learns quickly and turns quickly". It is important that all members of the regiment and the British public should understand the Gurkha ethos, which is "from the roots [do] not judge, but from the fruits". All Gurkha soldiers are not recruited from the hills any more. People right across Nepal, outside the hill districts, are now just as familiar with the British and amenable to them. Nepal has been influenced by Western culture and the Nepalese imitate Western life very quickly. There were no discos in my time in Nepal. I went to a disco for the first time in 1984 when my unit moved from Hong Kong to the UK.'

So, here we have one of Professor Caplan's 'romantic approvers' who is not a white British officer, but an ethnic Gurkha officer, who is just as passionate as his white counterparts in approving of what he considers to be the right things. Here we have an authentic Gurkha voice that sounds very much like those of white officers. According to his perspective – not theirs – ethnic Gurkha soldiers are unique, as is their regimental ethos.

But, in the opinion of this authentic Gurkha voice, there are other things besides that are not generally voiced by white British officers, even in the most recent books about Gurkha soldiers. In Laxmi's opinion the 'other person' in today's Gurkha soldier is a visionary who is better educated, skilled and more intelligent than before. He learns quickly and may no longer be from the original Gorkha tribes. He is a modern Nepalese who likes to swing in discos and he knows much more about Western culture. He is less of a wild boy from the hills – he may not be from the hills at all – but he remains no less brave and tough for all that and he is as proud and committed to the old military ethos as his ancestors were. Clearly, from this Gurkha perspective, the Gurkha man behind the military image has changed dramatically and will doubtless continue to do so. And, for the first time in military books about him, he is also intelligent, educated and cultured.

But what of the Nepalese Gurkha perspective on the British soldier?

'One of the best fighting soldiers in the world. I am not just saying that. It is well-known and I certainly believe it,' says Laxmi.

Laxmi also still believes that Nepalese Gurkha soldiers are, 'in the words of Professor Sir Ralph Turner [who served with the 3rd Queen Alexandra's own Gurkha Rifles during the First World War], "the bravest of the brave, most generous of the generous, never had a country more faithful friends than you".'

This flattering and well-deserved assessment of his Gurkha soldiers from a white British officer and a distinguished academic is wholeheartedly shared by an ethnic Gurkha officer in the new millennium.

I put it to Laxmi that perhaps the British and Nepalese fighting men who serve in the same regiments have become like clones who, despite their racial differences and the different colour of their skins, have come to resemble each other more and more, because they are on the same wavelength and programmed in the same way. Aren't soldiers all over the world cast in the same mould, speaking the same language, whatever their differences of culture and mother tongue?

He says: 'The Gurkhas are like the British in one way, but not in another. They are different with regard to religious matters, culture, customs, language and way of life. This means that, if any problems arise in the ranks, Gurkhas must solve them in their own way, not in the British way. But the two races are surprisingly alike when it comes to collective hard work and fighting against the enemy.'

It is certainly true, as Laxmi says, that Gurkhas must be allowed to solve problems in the ranks in their own way and that they cannot be treated like their British counterparts. It's no good shouting, screaming and swearing at them, or trying to humiliate them, because that doesn't work in the Gurkha culture. And it's no good interfering with their very civilised eating arrangements, as we have already heard from Major Mark Austin.

A reminder of these differences between the ways of

Gurkha and British soldiers was provided by an incident in Hawaii in 1986 involving a white British commanding officer on secondment to the Gurkhas from the Royal East Anglian Regiment. Not having absorbed the all-important Gurkha ethos to which Laxmi Bantawa refers, or understood that things are done differently in the Gurkhas, Major Corin Pearce soon found that he had lost the trust and respect of his men, without which no officer can do anything with the Gurkhas. According to Gurkha Lance Corporal Prakash Sunuwar (quoted in Tony Gould's *Imperial Warriors*), Pearce apparently said on a BBC documentary film for American viewers that Gurkhas come: 'From the hills, they don't have homes, they are not educated, they don't get adequate food, they cannot wear shoes. They work for us because of their poverty. Now look how we have trained them up.' And according to those who have spoken to Professor Caplan about this (in his book *Warrior Gentlemen*), the Gurkhas were not happy in their relationship with Pearce and spoke back to him 'in anger, and made trouble. They beat him. Whoever is put down will be angry. If you come here and I put you down, will you be angry or not?'

This strong aversion to even the suggestion of being humiliated reflects the sensitive Gurkha-Nepalese temperament, rather than that of the British, because the relatively insensitive latter often put one another down, particularly in the armed forces. In fact, in the thick-skinned British Army it is very much part of the training for soldiers to be sworn at and even humiliated by their superiors. It makes no difference to them because they learn not to take it to heart. But it goes against the grain with both white and ethnic Gurkha officers. Maybe paternalism is long gone in Gurkha regiments – and more's the pity, some say – but to dance on the grave of that paternalism is vulgar and foolhardy in the extreme, and the mind boggles at the prospect of a British Gurkha officer, even on secondment (how did he get in, in the first place?), allegedly doing such a monstrous thing.

In *Imperial Warriors*, Gould tells us that the mutinous Gurkha soldiers in Hawaii had 'a number of complaints: about the quantity and quality of the rice they were given, the level of overseas allowances and the fact that all available vehicles were monopolised by the "white officers" so that they had to walk to and from the camp, with the result that, as L/Cpl Prakash Sunuwar told a *Sunday Times* reporter: "When we would come back late, the mess would be closed and there would be no food." In addition to these gripes, they had taken offence at remarks Major Corin Pearce had apparently made... Things came to a head at a party to celebrate the conclusion of the joint exercise with units of the US 25th Infantry Division. The company commander made a heavy-handed attempt to stop the men drinking; but since they had contributed towards the cost of the party, they resented his interference and returned to the camp in a dangerously disgruntled mood... They surged forward and knocked him [Captain Chandra Pradhan] unconscious... Major Pearce had also been attacked and was now having his head stitched in the medical centre ... some fifteen stitches... on arrival in Hong Kong, the entire company was herded into wire cages on the backs of trucks and generally treated as criminals ...

while attempts were made to discover the ringleaders… Faced with this sort of witch hunt, the Gurkhas closed ranks and withheld co-operation, precipitating their dismissal *en masse*; in the end, 120 men were sent back to Nepal.'

Such handling of Gurkha soldiers has never been characteristic of Britain's Gurkha regiments (come back paternalism, all is forgiven!). But it may be that this is a sign, not only of changing times, but also of cutbacks in the British Army, which apparently accepts these days that white Gurkha officers who are not sufficiently enthusiastic or paternalistic to stay on with their Gurkha soldiers, or to learn their language and respect their different ways, are nevertheless fit to command them. If this is so, it represents a break with history and a painful wrench away from the best Gurkha traditions.

The infamous Hawaii incident throws a harsh new light of gritty realism on the sort of literature which has presented Gurkha soldiers as, according to Caplan, 'the "pet," ever loyal and obedient' or as 'gambolling bull-pups' and 'human and dog-like at the same time' in their 'devotion' to their officers. Far from being 'transformed into pets', the Gurkhas may be presented quite differently in present-day and future books about them. As, indeed, may their white British officers. In the absence of a strong Gurkha tradition and empathy in the British Army in future years, a new breed of British officers may come to lose the knack of leading Gurkhas, and to forget that loyalty and devotion have to be earned by example and leadership. Unless, of course, they return to the long-forgotten paternalism of earlier years that seemed to work its magic on generations of Gurkha soldiers.

But back to Laxmi Bantawa, who has the image of a very modern native Gurkha officer. With his smiling, kindly face and softly spoken manner, he comes over as a gentle soul. Yet he is a Gurkha paratrooper and carries a *kukri*. Like so many Gurkha soldiers, he has that baby-faced, clean-cut, boyish look. I ask him if he thinks that the Gurkhas' *kukri*-wielding image dehumanises them in any way.

'No, it doesn't. The Gurkha draws his *kukri* as a last resort when there are no other options. Once drawn, either he chops the enemy, or he dies for the rest of his comrades. The *kukri* is our traditional weapon and very few Gurkhas need to be taught about its use. Gurkhas always feel safe, fearless and confident when they carry their *kukri* on their waist. I personally prefer to carry a *kukri* rather than a bayonet.'

Laxmi joined the Gurkhas at nineteen years of age 'but officially recorded as eighteen, in 1976', from the hill village of Selejung in the Oyam region, which is in the Panchthar district. He was born in 1956 and his father was a farmer. He tells me that 'there was no village school when I was born', but when the first school opened its doors, in 1961, Laxmi went 'eagerly into it at five years of age, after having learnt the Nepalese alphabet at home'.

There he discovered that his 'best subject was maths' and he also learnt English. His father equipped him with a large and unwieldy blackboard with a handle – 'known as a Pati in Nepal' – that he carried around with him whenever he went to school. This was 'because there was no writing paper, other than occasional sheets of wrapping paper which my father tore from large packets of cotton wool imported from India.

But this wrapping paper was no good at all, so I stuck to my blackboard in the absence of proper exercise books.'

There surely cannot be any white British officer in the forces today, or in recent times, who had no school exercise books or paper, and had to carry a blackboard and chalk around with him each day instead.

Having reached the rank of major, Laxmi has done very well for himself, and he says that he is 'able to send money back to Nepal' from his home at the Shorncliffe barracks, so that he can 'provide for my father and three brothers and five sisters including their children'. (Sadly, Laxmi's mother died last year.)

Again, there cannot be any white British officers in the armed forces today having to support so many people out of their pay.

Laxmi 'owns two houses in Nepal, one in Kathmandu, the other in Dharan'.

When Laxmi was a child, his father 'farmed rice, corn and millet up in the hills. There were two buffaloes for milk, one bull, about a dozen goats, some chicken and pigs, so we could eat well. The pigs were fattened up for Dashain – which is our equivalent of your Christmas – and I was happy enough, even though life was very hard. I would often walk for twelve days through the eastern hills to the nearest shop to get salt for my parents – six days each way, sleeping rough – and sometimes I had to go as far as Darjeeling, across the border into India, which was a fourteen-day journey, with ten kilos of salt on the return journey, carried on my back in a basket – or in a *dhakar*, very similar to a *dhoko*, as we say in our language. We paid 20p for ten kilos of salt in those days and 20p was worth quite a lot at that time. I did not see a bus until I was sixteen years of age when I went to Dharan to get the salt. When I took my first bus journey, I was worried that the vehicle's construction was too rigid and upright, so I wondered if it would fall over when going round our winding hillside roads and mountain passes!'

While his father had never been a soldier, Laxmi says that his mother's father was a Gurkha, 'retired as a Subedar in 1947 from India, and this inspired me to join the Gurkhas. Also, my mother's brother was a Gurkha who died in World War Two and this captured my imagination.' Things were not so very different in Britain in those far-off days after the Second World War, when there was no end of retired soldiers on the streets and park benches right across the country, including many of my neighbours and relatives in my home town, Reading. Two of my mother's brothers were retired, from the Brigade of Guards and the Indian Cavalry respectively, while my brother was demobbed from the Lancashire Fusiliers and my father's brother from the Parachute Regiment.

Laxmi continues: 'I decided at fifteen years of age that I would apply to the Gurkhas when I left school at nineteen, after I had learnt English a little. It seemed to be the best form of employment. The Gurkha soldiers who came home on Nepal leave or pension always looked fit, smart and clean, and they had nice clothes and money in their pockets. I went straight from school into the Gurkhas, to Hong Kong for nine months. I have served in many countries, such as Brunei, the USA, Malaysia, Bosnia, Canada, the Gulf, Hawaii and Croatia with different Gurkha units. I was also at the Gurkha recruit-training centre at Catterick Garrison in Yorkshire and I saw action during the Gulf War. I certainly think the British Army is the best in the world and within the British Army the Gurkhas are great and unique. I have spent twenty-six years with the regiment and have had a much better life than I would have done if I had stayed in the eastern hills of Nepal. The British Army has been my whole life. It has given me everything. All my family are proud of it.'

No doubt there are plenty of people in Nepal today who regret that they can no longer join the Gurkhas now that the British Army is shrinking fast. Talking politics now, Laxmi tells me that the situation in Nepal is currently: 'Very fragile and painful to the public. During the last six years more than 4,000 have been killed, including security forces, politicians, teachers and innocent civilians. I have heard that communist rebels come at night to demand food and money and they kill those who do not give. If there is no food or money, they demand one son or daughter who must go and fight for them. When the parents give in to the rebels, in order to save their own skins, then the government agencies come the next day and put pressure on them for supporting the rebels! The rebels are using the public in the front line as a human shield.

'The government security forces do not understand the plight of the poor people. The army is not sufficiently mobile to fight the rebels in the hills – they also need to guard the palace and other key locations – and it doesn't have sufficient logistical support to sustain operations. Daily I hear from my friends and those who come back from Nepal. The problem in

Nepal today is that the public is weak and defenceless; there is too much corruption. Law and order and leadership are very poor. The government forces do not know how to win the hearts and minds of the public, while the royal family is also in a difficult situation. The present king and government are trying very hard to put it back together. Two-thirds of the people are of Mongolian descent and one-third of Indian origin. China says that it is not supporting the present problem, but some say that their hidden hand is behind the Maoists. China has very little appeal to most Nepalese because of the geographical situation. China is cut off by the mountains to the north and there is only one road between Nepal and China, the Ariniko Highway.

'But Nepal has an open-border policy with India and lots of roads going south. Nepalese people much prefer Indian music, television, radio, Bollywood films, newspapers and food, and there is a big Indian community living in Nepal, where many of the merchants are Indian. There are five main roads going into Nepal's hills and mountains, with most of the roads to the eastern hills. The West is wider and more remote than the East, and that is where most of the communist rebels come from. Hills such as Rukum, Rolpa, Jajarkot and Kalikot are remote places in the West where it takes two to three days' walk to reach them. The three top leaders of the rebels' party are all of upper Indian descent. It is said that the aim of the rebels is to overthrow the monarchy and the government by 2006.'

Although he cannot personally vouch for the total accuracy of these reports, Laxmi says that he is certainly inclined to believe them, and he explains: 'This is the message that I get from my friends. The government has announced cash rewards of five million rupees on the heads of each of the top rebel leaders.'

Laxmi hopes to retire to Nepal when he has served his time, provided that there are no insurmountable problems there. With recent improvements in pay and pensions for Gurkha soldiers and officers, 'there is more than enough for us to live on if we settle in the hills – most of the ex-servicemen are very happy with their pensions and it is very sad that some are saying otherwise and pursuing this in the courts.'

On the subject of recent 'provocative' newspaper reports about the Royal Gurkha Rifles that have appeared in Britain's *Daily Mirror* – beginning on 29 April 2002 in an article entitled 'The Most Appalling Form of Colonial Racism Imaginable' – Laxmi disagrees with their suggestions of racism against Gurkha soldiers by officers in their command. He says that 'it's simply not true that Gurkha officers have to salute junior British officers, and I might say that when I salute any officer, it is the Queen's Commission that I am saluting, not him. It is out of respect for myself, not out of deference to another officer. Every soldier and officer is supposed to know that. I can honestly say that I am not aware of any racism in the ranks.'

Talking to Laxmi, one is reminded that we in the West have lost something vital, despite all the other gains that we have made in our progressive societies. We moan and groan and get angry about all manner of trivial things, complaining of injustice, disadvantage and a hard life, when we wouldn't recognise a hard life if it jumped up and bit us in the bum. Yet here is a Gurkha officer who has been bitten in the bum from a very young age, and is he complaining? Is he hell! He isn't complaining because in Nepal there was no point, and these days he cannot see the point. He understands that all of the painful obstacles that he and his fellow Gurkha soldiers have had to overcome are what have made them who and how they are, lending considerably to their charm, and that turning life's defects into virtues is the name of the game. He is cheerful, uncomplaining and calm, philosophically accepting everything that life chucks at him. Of course, one doesn't want to romanticise these Gurkhas too much, but one would have to be a very mean-spirited and self-regarding person not to recognise the beauty of such an approach to life, which provides us with an alternative outlook to that of most people in the West today.

Compared with the 'larger than life', touchy-feely and self-indulgent wimps and celebs who are 'romantically approved' and presented on our television screens today – from the 'perspective' of those programmers and audience-ratings men who want them to cry for the camera and go bananas punching the air for the slightest accomplishment or triumph – the Laxmi Bantawas of this world do not seem all that exaggerated. Compared with the banal values of present-day TV soap opera, they seem equally deserving.

Anybody who is interested in what Professor Caplan calls 'examining the link between the word and the world' should talk to Laxmi Bantawa. And should they believe that most Gurkha texts 'mourn the loss not simply of what is no more, but what has never existed', they should talk to him about that too. Caplan is not unaware of 'the relativity of objectivity' (what you see depends on who you are) and there can be no doubt that what he sees is not what the Laxmi Bantawas of this world see, because the professor has not been where Laxmi has been or done and suffered what he has done and suffered (nor has the professor been where the white British officer class have been as they have 'moulded the discourse and authored the literature on the Gurkhas'). The professor complains of 'a woeful absence of dialogue between them [the Gurkhas] and British officers who produce the literature of the Gurkhas' on behalf of the people who have loyally followed their officers 'to hell and back'. The chances are that this book is the first to correct that situation. This is because it contains a dialogue between ethnic Gurkha officers and their white British counterparts, in the sense that interviews on- and off-record with ethnic Gurkhas on the subject of their white officers (as well as on military and political affairs) may be read in juxtaposition to interviews with British officers featured elsewhere in the text.

Future writers on the Gurkhas will need to talk to ethnic Gurkha and Nepalese soldiers more and more if they are to breathe new life into the story of a fighting force that has been written about more than most units of the British Army, including its forces in India. Future books may also need to pay more attention to what Laxmi Bantawa describes as the 'internal component of the Gurkha' and the Gurkha *kaida* (regimental customs, methods and traditions), for as Gurkha numbers dwindle within the ranks, their *kaida* is easily overlooked (it stands to reason that, if you have a lot of Gurkha soldiers under your command, you are much more mindful of their racial and cultural differences than you are with just a few such soldiers to think about).

Whether or not we agree with everything that Major Bantawa says about the Gurkhas, we can see exactly what his perspective is and where he is coming from. We are not reliant on his white British officers for our view of him. His is a fascinating story honestly told from his own predictable perspective, point of view and personal experience. In listening to this ethnic Gurkha voice, we see him as an 'aware' human being as well as a soldier; we glimpse the man behind the regimental persona. He is, of course, a Gurkha success story, but, for a change, a brown-faced rather than a white-faced success, given his own head to tell his own story, rather than being portrayed through the words of white British officers.

I am grateful to him for his time and co-operation and hope that he will enjoy reading his interview as much as I have enjoyed writing and interpreting it.

*An Outline History of the Brigade of Gurkhas*, issued by the Gurkha Museum in Winchester, includes the following quotation from Field Marshal Sir William Slim: 'I first met the Gurkha Rifles in Gallipoli. There I was so struck by their bearing in one of the most desperate battles in history that I resolved, should the opportunity come, to try to serve with them. Four years later it came, and I spent many of the happiest, and from a military point of view the most valuable, years of my life in the Regiment.'

This was Slim's perception – romanticised or otherwise, it makes no difference – of his first impressions of the Gurkhas and, later on, of the happy and valuable times that he feels that he had with them. It is odd, to say the least, to describe his consciousness of his exposure to the Gurkhas as something that, in reality, 'never was'.

Of course it was and of course Gurkha soldiers are. They are not fictions as they live up to their reputation for larger-than-life adventure, heroism and loyalty.

Their and their white officers' perceptions are at least as valid as those of academics and others.

# eleven

# BETTER TO DIE THAN BE A COWARD

Not all of us would agree with the proud motto of the Brigade of Gurkhas: 'Better to die than to be a coward.'

There are even some Gurkha soldiers and officers who have not agreed, as Birdie Smith makes clear in his book *Even the Brave Falter*. Birdie Smith is a white British Gurkha officer and his book was described by the *British Army Review* as 'one of the most honest books ever written by a soldier' and as 'a valuable study of leadership and morale in battle' by *The Army Quarterly*.

Brigadier Smith's sensitive book deals with the complicated nature of courage, raising interesting questions for all Gurkha soldiers and officers, past and present, the majority of whom are expected to be in complete agreement with the rule of conduct enshrined in their motto.

If we must have wars, this shining ideal seems to make perfect sense. But do those who must decide between cowardice and courage when war looms, really have any choice in the matter? Most of us would agree that there's no point sending mummy's boys into battle and then expecting such boys to keep our enemies at bay, and that there's absolutely no point at all in keeping a cowardly guard dog that takes fright when a burglar comes prowling. But where does this refusal to be a coward come from and how reliable is it?

While the Gurkhas are rightly famed around the world for their bravery, there are some important exceptions, as Birdie Smith's book makes clear. Even Gurkhas are not always as brave as they would wish, and some discover that occasionally they lack courage when they most need it. Not many, note, but some.

But, so what if not all of these guys are superhuman? Who is? Well, it can make the difference between winning and losing a battle, that's what.

Yet even the less than brave can be induced to conquer their fear and rise to great feats of bravery, which is where the Gurkhas believe that their motto comes in. In *Even the Brave Falter* there are old and young Gurkha soldiers and officers who lose their nerve and find it difficult, even impossible, to rise to the challenge (and this, of course, happens in all regiments and armies, all over the world). Smith's book discusses the fickle nature of courage and the insidious infection of fear – especially when troops, officers and men are inexperienced. In the first chapter of this book,

Colonel Dawson of the Royal Gurkha Rifles echoed Birdie Smith's dismissal of the Gurkhas' supposed bloodlust, and I have heard similar denials from other British Gurkha officers. Even so, it is when the Gurkhas are roused that they are at their fighting rather than their caring best, and it is this that has captured the public imagination, and for which they are best known and remembered in the minds of most of their enemies and admirers alike. There are jokes about the Argentinians' fear of the Gurkhas during the Falklands War, where, finding themselves running towards the Gurkhas, they are said to have turned tail and run straight into the arms of the British Paras instead, believing them to be the lesser of the evils (some hope!). Argentinians pleaded with the Paras not to be left in the care of Gurkhas. When you consider how the cowardly Argentinians mistreated their British civilian prisoners when they first invaded the Falklands, the brave and necessarily brutal Gurkhas emerge as much more civilised. It doesn't follow that the cowardly are more caring, or more civilised and less cruel, when they have people at their mercy. On the contrary, they can become very cruel, since they know, in their hearts, that they are unmanly and cowardly. They can take out all their violence and aggression on their captives, because they are not brave enough to take it out on others more brave than they.

But there have been occasions when even some of the brave Gurkhas have been let down badly by their courage. Birdie Smith tells us that the 'fickle nature of courage' is likely to show itself when men are inexperienced and liable to panic when the unexpected happens (for this reason, professional soldiers are always putting their bravery to the test, preparing themselves in advance and sorting the men from the boys.) Smith also comments on a Gurkha soldier who lost his nerve during the Second World War and was given a dishonourable discharge for failing to live up to the proud Gurkha motto.

The extent to which people need to be brave – and whether, in fact, bravery is a good or even a necessary thing – is a question that must occur to all but the most bravery-crazed or moronic. I have always taken the view that people either are or are not brave and that there is nothing much that they can do about it. They can no more help being brave than they can help being cowardly, because it is a nervous condition that suddenly comes over them and decides the matter for them. So it is largely out of their hands and they cannot take too much credit for their bravery (or shame for their cowardice). Some would seem to have much braver genes than others, which is why people should not be ashamed of being cowardly.

Nobody in their right mind wants to be an out-and-out coward, or perhaps even unduly brave, if they can help it, but it really does seem that most people just cannot help themselves. Most people know that some of us 'do' bravery much better than others, or at least are better than others at overcoming cowardly feelings, just as most people realise that there are others who are much more concerned than the rest of us with exploring and displaying their bravery by regularly putting it to the test.

When I say that nobody of sound mind wants to be unduly brave, I am not suggesting that bravery does not have its uses, or that cowardice is a splendid thing (although both these things can be a part of a person's charm). But there is no point in being *stupidly* brave.

It so happens that, while I was doing my national service in Cyprus, at nineteen years of age, in 1960, I chickened out of the needless bravery required to live up to the motto of the Royal Corps of Signals, which was *Certa Cito* (Swift and Sure). I am attracted to the ideal of being swift and sure and this motto is certainly one that appeals to me; not that I have ever been the sort who follows mottoes or orders slavishly (on the contrary, I have always been one of those who believes that orders are for the guidance of wise men and the obedience of fools). As one of a patrol that was sent up into the mountains to smoke out any remaining Greek terrorists at the end of the troubles in Cyprus, I got into an argument with a couple of Glaswegian signalmen when we suspected that we might have detected a terrorist hideaway, high above us on top of an overhanging cliff, under which we had taken shelter from the sun in a cave. The Jocks were all for scrambling up the cliff face, which offered no cover, to see if there were any terrorists at the top, despite the fact that, if there were terrorists there, then their snipers would surely pick us off with no trouble (the chief tactic of the Greek Cypriot terrorists in Cyprus in those days was to snipe, ambush, bomb and shoot unsuspecting soldiers in the back, not to come out and fight them fair and square).

I was already under the impression that these two Jocks

were as thick as planks, but this was by far the most stupid thing I had heard from their lips in a long time, so I did my best to point out, without reference to their obvious dimness, that they would be sitting ducks, that it would be better to find some other route where cover was available to us. This resulted in a tirade of abuse from the impatient Jocks, who called me a feeble coward, to which I replied that I was not feeling particularly feeble or cowardly, and that only a complete moron would risk his life in the manner that they were proposing. But for what purpose? Just to see if we could catch a few more terrorists before demob (which was getting closer by the week)? Far better, I insisted, to find another route to the top of the cliff, instead of risking our lives needlessly in a futile act of bravery, thereby putting ourselves at the mercy of terrorists who would surely consider themselves far less stupid than us as they shot us dead. Far better, if there were terrorists overhead, to let them come for us and put themselves at risk.

But the Jocks would hear nothing of it and they reminded me that our motto was 'Swift and Fucking Sure', not 'Dithering and Slow'! So off they went up the cliff without me, fully exposed to enemy gunfire from above. As things turned out, they were in luck, because there were no terrorists at the top of the cliff (perhaps they had become bored, run out of patience and moved on while we argued!), but there could have been, and two British soldiers could have been dead and returned to Glasgow in body bags. Instead of which they escaped with their lives and thought themselves brave and worthy soldiers.

We are reminded by these experiences of the mindless lengths to which some people will go merely to prove that, perish the thought, they are definitely not cowards, and to avoid the stigma or slur of cowardice.

But it's one thing to sensibly withhold one's courage, without fear of being branded a coward (to be brave enough to be called a coward) and until the time is right and needful, and quite another thing entirely to find one's courage desperately lacking when one most needs it. Smith tells us that: 'Such things happened to the bravest, to the best: something snapped so that the individual's deposit of courage dried up, ceased to function. Some called it battle fatigue, others gave it names cruelly descriptive of those unfortunate men who could no longer withstand the strain and stresses of fighting.'

It doesn't follow from these judgements that those men were not brave, or that they were necessarily cowards. And Smith was with a battalion whose 'Gurkhas are terrific in attack and are usually given the toughest nut to crack. Considering that they come from a country which is not in the Empire, do not know who or what Hitler is, or even care, their spirit and willingness to fight for the British is incredible... I was not the first or last British officer to be moved to write in such terms about his beloved Gurkha soldiers.'

This 'incredible' Gurkha spirit and willingness to fight for the imperial British, of all people, is the clearest evidence of the romantic and platonic love affair that has continued to this day between these two martial races. That is why so many British Gurkha officers have been moved to write in such admiring and glowing terms about their Gurkha soldiers, and that is why the Gurkhas never failed to come up trumps for the British.

Having talked with Gurkha soldiers and officers on my travels in different parts of the world, having done research and interviews for this book and having listened to the things that British soldiers from other units have to say, in gratitude and admiration, about the Gurkhas wherever they have seen them in action in the service of the British Crown, I can in no way fault the relationship in military, human or political terms. The Gurkhas have their place in British hearts and that's all there is to it.

These days a lot of people worry that, when talking about war and honouring crack troops and glamorous regiments, we are glorying in carnage and encouraging the mad dogs. But they are not necessarily mad dogs, most of these men, who can somehow live with the deaths of others on their conscience, so that we can sleep safely in our beds, and who do not see themselves as murderers but as being brave enough to stand up to murderers. And if some of them do occasionally want a little glory from what they do, we cannot expect brave men to put their lives on the line for us and then refuse to acknowledge our debt to them, or refuse to pay tribute to their courage and heroism, without which we are lost. If a little glory is what makes them tick, or compensates them for what we have put them through on our behalf, who are we to say no to that glory when we say yes to the rest? How can we expect them to undertake the gruesome business of war on our behalf, and then behave as if they have done nothing very special, as if they don't deserve our special thanks, or perhaps even our admiration?

If we must go to war, it is churlish and graceless in the extreme not to honour our men of war and to praise them accordingly. That doesn't mean to say that we give them a blank cheque, or romanticise them so that we lose sight of the ugly reality of war. What it means is simply that we respect and thank them, that's all. We should not be too embarrassed or too ungrateful and ungracious to honour them once in a while. Since wars are a fact of life, we may as well face up to them and not sell short the men on whom we always call to fight these wars for us. As Smith points out: 'Although our nation was at peace, British servicemen were on active service every year [since 1945] except 1968, the year in which this story ends.'

What is puzzling to many people is why some feel obliged to become soldiers, why they feel that they are born to be fighting men and to protect the rest of us who feel nothing of the kind? What would they find to do with their aggression, if there was peace everywhere and nothing needed to be protected any more? What is it about them that they apparently need a war to fight? Such people feel, with good reason, that wars are an *unacceptable* fact of life – and soldiers too – but wars don't go away just because that's how we feel about them. They come and go regardless of whether or not we glory in them and, when they come, we have to redress the terrible wrongs to which they give rise, otherwise there is no hope at all for us – only for the bully boys, the evil and the aggressors.

I am reminded of the words of Spike Milligan quoted in Cecil Woolf and Jean Moorcroft Wilson's *Authors Take Sides on the Falklands*: 'the only way to end wars is to have them.'

Anyone who thinks that, by praising Gurkha soldiers, we are encouraging the mad dogs of war, should read Birdie Smith. In the preface to his book *Wars Bring Scars*, he quotes Samuel Butler's *Hudibras*: 'There's but the twinkling of a star/Between a man of peace and war', and he goes on to say 'this is not a book that glorifies the infrequent bouts of "Active Service" in which I participated … the 1964 walk in the valley of the shadow of death did not change my attitude to soldiering – which was to stop war, not to make it. A young, Left-wing journalist once asked me if I had a conscience about anyone who might have been killed by the soldiers under my command. My reply was: "No, because for anyone we might have killed, there were dozens of lives we saved"… My Gurkha soldiers put their lives on the line for this country: the scars some of us received would not deter them, or myself from doing the same again if given a second chance.' ('Doing the same again', one is tempted to observe, for left-wing journalists and other critics of the military.)

The refreshing thing about reading Birdie Smith is that he deals with cowardice and courage in human terms – realistically and honestly – and without gilding the lily or in any way glorying in war. For a balanced and mature view of this subject and the Gurkhas' famous motto, his books are essential reading, not only for future recruits, but for all who write about and comment on these deeply emotive and prejudiced matters.

# twelve

# THE LAUGHING GURKHAS

The Gurkhas like to laugh. Everybody says so. Humour is an essential part of their make-up. Of all the things that characterise Gurkha soldiers, laughter is chief among them. Their humour and ability to laugh in the face of adversity has been mentioned by their white British officers from one generation to the next, from the novelist John Masters in the earlier part of the twentieth century to Major Mark Austin and Colonel Dawson in the new millennium, the latter of whom are extensively quoted in this book.

In *Imperial Warriors*, the former Gurkha officer Tony Gould mentions Gurkha humour four times, and he summarises as follows: 'Recognition of a shared sense of the ridiculous was (and is) the great bond between British and Gurkha soldiers ... first and foremost ... is the Gurkha sense of humour… a quick sense of the ridiculous that spared no one, neither the Colonel, themselves, nor me.'

Having put humour at the top of the list of Gurkha qualities, Gould expands: 'Then there is their honesty … a natural integrity, an inborn frankness. Courage comes only third because it seems to me not so uncommon, though I acknowledge that a people without courage are nothing… Courage, said our General Slim, "is like having money in the bank. It is an expendable quality." Finally there is the tenacity for which Gurkhas are famous.'

So then, humour above courage and tenacity, because it is a rarer quality. It is distinctively a Gurkha trait, and this is much to their credit. (On the debit side, Gould reckons that Gurkha traits include such things as womanising, gambling and drinking strong liquor, and these too are not entirely devoid of humour.) Gould gives us an interesting example of Gurkha humour at its most subtle. When, up in the hills of Nepal in recent times, rival gangs of young men were creating a public nuisance by arming themselves with sticks and *kukris* and threatening one another, they were summoned by Gurung village elders and a policeman to a public meeting. They were not lectured on the evils of violence or fighting, but simply told that they 'were hopelessly disorganized, barging around like alarmed elephants … they needed a proper plan of battle. And so on… when ex-Gurkhas went on to offer their own services as officers the youngsters muttered something about thinking it over and slunk away. The old soldiers had made their point and there was no more trouble after that. One of them … shrugged it off as a simple matter of "reverse psychology"… What I like about this story is that it reveals the wit and wisdom of the Gurung *lahores* [soldiers of fortune] in their home environment and shows them using their military experience imaginatively to defuse a potentially explosive social situation. It makes me laugh and, at the same time, it makes me proud ever to have been associated with such a people.'

Adults and old soldiers used to perform this sort of social function in Britain until the fifties, but not any more, alas. The streets and public parks were full of former soldiers and sailors who had seen plenty of action and had no fear of aggressive young men in need of role models or discipline. Today such socially disruptive and criminal youths are indeed lectured on the evils of violence and fighting and they are sometimes sympathised with for having had an unhappy childhood after they have beaten an old lady to a pulp and put her into hospital, gang-raped a woman, or given a defenceless young man a kicking, or perhaps stabbed him to death, after ganging up on him for the purpose. They are told that they have rights and are not beyond redemption. What these cowardly and violent young men need, of course, is for some wily and humorous old soldiers to offer to sort them out in a friendly fashion, to deflate their egos by wittily implying that they are unmanly. They need to be cut down to size by being told, in good Gurkha style, that they are, like their counterparts in the hills of Nepal, 'like alarmed elephants'.

Like their British masters, the Gurkhas enjoy a good laugh and they know how to laugh in the face of adversity and danger. They are at home with humour and can see the funny side of life. It is part of their charm and their strength of character. If they have iron in their souls, they also have humour in their heads and hearts. And this too – in addition to their other soldierly qualities – has attracted Gurkha and British men of war to each other. It is this that has contributed in no small way to the ongoing love affair between these unlikely bedfellows who are otherwise very different.

But laughter as a soldierly quality? How come?

Well, if you can laugh in the face of adversity, danger and death itself, you have a better chance of not giving in to these things, and indeed of surviving them and winning through. Laughter provides the emotional and mental relief that can see you through, that can comfort you when you are on the verge of cracking up. It helps you not to feel sorry for yourself and, instead, to make the best of a bad job (and what is war if not a very bad job indeed?). Of course, you have to believe in laughter in the first place, in order to realise this, and not all races want to believe it. Some would seem to have a policy against it, whereas the British and Gurkhas have, for the most part, both in and out of military service, a very strong policy in favour of laughter.

I am not talking about being slick, joky and wisecracking, turning everything into a silly joke because you are not intellectually equipped to be serious. Nor am I talking about inanely making fun of people and things when they ought to be taken seriously. On the contrary, I am talking about the serious business of humour – the intellectual purpose of laughter.

If you are suffering from hardship and/or war wounds, fear

and physical exhaustion, or have fallen into the hands of a cruel enemy and become a prisoner, then humour is the best medicine. When you are without hope, or are troubled by fear, a good laugh makes all the difference in the world. When you are stressed out, or freaked out, laugher can come to your aid. Maybe the military authorities should teach this. But, then again, there's not much point for British and Gurkha recruits, because they will know this already, most of them, coming as they do from countries in which there is a long tradition of humour.

It is a mystery why some races have more humour and enjoy laughing out loud more than others – why the British, Irish, Americans, Australasians and Jews are known for their humour when others are not. I am not talking about nervous or embarrassed laughter, or laughing silently and guiltily to oneself, for fear of upsetting somebody's applecart. Everybody does that from time to time. I am talking about taking unashamed humour in one's stride and having a culture and philosophy of life in which laughter is generally approved and openly encouraged as a good thing most of the time. This is humour as a matter of policy and it includes both humour that comes naturally, and other forms of humour that are invented by witty minds to trigger laughter in others to whom it might not come naturally, to help them to see the funny side of things.

It is evident that British soldiers and their Gurkha comrades have a sense of humour in common, and that they have used humour to transcend their racial differences and to survive battles. There has always been a strong tradition of laughter in both cultures, and this is doubtless another of the reasons why the two races have taken such a shine to each other, why the famous relationship has lasted so long. But there is another point too: laughter as a weapon of war can come in handy. It is very good for morale, for keeping spirits and chins up when they might otherwise be down. People with a good sense of humour will have a good fighting spirit as well. Satirising and lampooning the enemy; making fun or light of the enemy; making fun or light of one's own wounds, suffering and fears; making fun of life and death and war itself; all this is part of the absurdist game in times of war which is, without doubt, the most absurd of all the ridiculous and atrocious games that humans play. In the case of war, laughter is the spoonful of sugar than makes a very bitter medicine go down. While laughing at the suffering of others – laughing at cripples or beggars – is in extremely bad taste, laughing at the enemy when he is making us suffer is definitely the thing to do.

Laughter as a means of bucking us up when we are down – compensating us for what we can never be, however much we try – and laughter as a form of cutting others down to size and reminding them that they are not as fearsome, clever or superior as they would like the rest of us to think that they are, is what goes into the making of a good sense of humour.

At the same time, if you can break the ice by laughing *with* someone, rather than *at* them, you can do all sorts of other things besides. And it is surely obvious that, in times of war, soldiers and civilians need all the humour they can get from those around them. Consider the words of a Bud Flanagan song that was popular during the Second World War:

*'Who do you think you're kidding, Mr Hitler*
*If you think Old England's done?*
*We are the boys who will stop your little game,*
*We are the boys who will make you think again.'*

Thinking again is what Hitler had to do (as did we all as a result of that war) and this and other humorous songs kept a lot of people going during the darkest hours of the Blitz. It kept them optimistic when wolfish pessimism was glaring them in the face and unspeakable defeat was tapping them on the shoulder. So what to do in the face of misery and possible defeat? Have a nervous breakdown? Surrender? Commit suicide? Or make up a funny song about something that is by no means funny?

A strong tradition of humour, with a readiness to laugh when the chips are down and one feels like crying, is chief among the attractive qualities that have brought Gurkha soldiers and their British officers together. It has contributed to the long-lasting relationship between the two and made these unlikely opposites into ideal partners through thick and thin.

It is natural not to want to laugh at oneself – to have a marked preference for laughing at others instead – and the acid test of an all-round sense of humour is whether or not we can laugh at ourselves. Soldiers so often can laugh at both themselves and others because, in the armed forces, there are many opportunities for people to laugh at themselves when they are stretched and challenged to the limit and all eyes are on them. As anyone who has done national service or been a professional soldier in Britain knows, there really is a laugh a minute for those with the humour to see it, among men from so many different social backgrounds and walks of life who never tire of having a go at one another with humour. In fact, it's almost impossible to survive military training without learning to laugh at oneself, secretly or openly, and developing a sense of adversarial humour.

There is much to suggest that the Gurkhas are very good at laughing at themselves (when they are not laughing at others). I am thinking in particular of the Gurkha who stuck his thumb in his pocket when it came off during a battle and long afterwards presented it to a doctor, asking if he could kindly stitch it back on again; the Gurkhas who, when cremating a respected colleague who had died on them, did not hesitate to leap into the flames when the corpse would not lie down, so that they could quickly flatten him out with their *kukris* and then getting out fast before going up in flames themselves, laughing as they did so (and having many a belly laugh about this afterwards); the Gurkhas who laughed at their superior officer, Major Mark Austin, when he fell into the camouflaged pit that they had dug in the jungle in order to catch wild pigs rather than an unfortunate British officer. These and so many other stories about Gurkha humour suggest that like their British comrades – but unlike Japanese soldiers, for example – they can laugh at themselves and are relaxed about laughing at others as well.

So, here's to the laughing Gurkhas! Long may they continue to laugh through thick and thin.

# SOURCES

## BOOKS

Caplan, Lionel, *Warrior Gentlemen – 'Gurkhas' in the Western Imagination* (Berghan Books, 1995)

Churchill, Winston, The World Crisis *(Odhams, 1939)*

Cross, John, *The Call of Nepal* (New Millennium, 1996)

Farrell, J.G., *The Siege of Krishnapur* (Flamingo, 1987)

Forster, E.M., A Passage to India *(Penguin, 1981)*

Fraser, James Baillie, *Journal of a Tour* (London, 1820) (quoted in Tony Gould's *Imperial Warriors*)

Gould, Tony, *Imperial Warriors* (Granta, 2000)

Hennessy, Peter, *Never Again* (Vintage, 1993)

Hopkirk, Peter, *The Great Game* (Oxford University Press, 2001)

Hunt, John, *The Ascent of Everest* (The Mountaineers, Seattle, USA, 1993)

Kipling, Rudyard, 'In The Presence' (Penguin, 1987)

Kitson Clark, G *The Critical Historian* (Heinemann, 1970)

Knightley, Phillip, *The First Casualty* (Quartet Books, 1982)

Lapping, Brian, *End of Empire* (Book Club Associates, 1985)

MacDonald Fraser, George, *Quartered Safe Out Here*
   (HarperCollins, 2000)

Marwick, Arthur, *War and Social Change in the 20th Century*
   (Macmillan, 1978)

*Matthews, Herbert,* The Education of a Correspondent
   *(Harcourt Brace, New York, 1946)*

Moorhouse, Geoffrey, *India Britannica* (Paladin, 1984)

Mudford, Peter, *The Art of Celebration* (Faber & Faber, 1979)

Rathaur, Kamal, *The British and the Brave: The Gurkhas, A
History of the Recruitment in the British Army*
   (Nirala Publications, Jaipur, 1987)

Rutherford, Andrew, *The Literature of War*
   (Macmillan, 1989)

Shipp, John, *The Path of Glory – The Memoirs of the
Extraordinary Career of John Shipp* (Chatto & Windus, 1969)

Slim, Field Marshal, *Defeat into Victory* (Cassell, 1956)

Smith, Birdie, *Johnny Gurkha* (Arrow Books, 1987)
   *Even The Brave Falter* (Robert Hale, 1980)
   *Wars Bring Scars* (R.J. Leach & Co, Ditton, Aylesford,
   Kent, 1993)

Warner, Philip, *Auchinleck – The Lonely Soldier*
   (Cassell, 2001)

Waugh, Evelyn, *Men at Arms* and *Officers and Gentlemen*,
   from *Sword of Honour* trilogy (Penguin, 1964)

Woodyat, Major General Nigel, *Under Ten Viceroys*
   (London, 1922)

SOURCES

Woolf, Cecil, and Moorcroft Wilson, Jean, *Authors Take Sides on the Falklands* (Cecil Woolf Publishers, 1982)


OTHER PUBLICATIONS

*An Account of the Kingdom of Nepal* (Asiatic Researches, Calcutta, 1790) by *Father Giuseppe* (quoted in Tony Gould's *Imperial Warriors*)

*An Outline History of the Brigade of Gurkhas* (Gurkha Museum, Winchester, 1999)

*Bugle & Kukri* (1999, 2001, 2002 editions)

Gurkha Museum Fact Sheet No 10, *The Northwest Frontier* (Gurkha Museum, Winchester, 1991)

*Historical Record of the 6th Gurkha Rifles* (National Army and Gurkha Museums)

*Daily Mirror*, 29 April 2002

*Flanagan, Bud, words from 'On The Air' (*Dad's Army *theme tune), in* 60 Years of BBC Theme Music, *BBC Records, 1982*

Internal Publications and Library, The Gurkha Museum, Winchester, Hampshire

*New York* magazine, 12 November 1973

*Sunday Times*, 20 April 1968


OTHER SOURCES

St James's Palace (quotations from HRH Prince Charles)

Royal Gurkha Rifles, Shorncliffe Barracks, Kent (information on portrait of Prince Charles and Delhi Table at Shorncliffe Barracks, Kent)